Sustained Through the Trials

Pat Robson

To Dear Hannah, With much love in Christ Jesus. God bless you, Pat R. xxx

Published by New Generation Publishing in 2015

Copyright © Pat Robson 2015

First Edition

The author asserts the moral right under the Copyright, Designs and Patents Act 1988 to be identified as the author of this work.

ISBN 978-1-78507-270-3

Scripture quotations are taken from the New International Version Holy Bible.

All Rights reserved. No part of this publication may be reproduced, stored in a retrieval system or transmitted, in any form or by any means without the prior consent of the author, nor be otherwise circulated in any form of binding or cover other than that which it is published and without a similar condition being imposed on the subsequent purchaser.

www.newgeneration-publishing.com

New Generation Publishing

CONTENTS

INTRODUCTION i
1. THE DIAGNOSIS 1
2. NO DESTINATION IN SIGHT 4
3. SHOCK AND HORROR 7
4. THE REUNION 10
5. LONGING FOR A FATHER'S LOVE 14
6. THE SHY PERFECTIONIST 17
7. HEALED OF ANGINA 19
8. THE SEARCH BEGINS 24
9. A SPIRITUAL HUNGER 29
10. GOD'S PROVISION 33
11. THE PROPHECY 36
12. ANSWER TO A CHILD'S PRAYER 39
13. WARNING 43
14. HOMELESS 48
15. EXHAUSTED BUT BLESSED 51
16. SO LITTLE YET SO MUCH 54
17. A FRIGHTENING ENCOUNTER 57
18. WORN AND WEARY 60
19. DEVASTATED 63
20. PURSUING A DIVORCE 66
21. THE JOY OF FAMILY WORSHIP 69
22. OVERWHELMED WITH JOY 72
23. BEREAVED 76
24. HARROWING SITUATIONS 79
25. ANSWERED PRAYER 83
26. ANOTHER MOVE 87
27. TOTAL DESPAIR 91
28. GOD'S FAITHFULNESS 95
29. MORE ANSWERED PRAYER 98
30. A BRAND NEW CAR 101
31. BACK TO UNIVERSITY 104
CONCLUSION 108

ACKNOWLEDGEMENTS

A special thanks to Dr. Derek Butters to whom I would be forever grateful for the encouragement he has given me in writing this book. His patient assistance and gentle unending support amidst his very busy itinerary was greatly appreciated.

I would also like to thank Sandra, a special friend whom I have known for many years and who has helped with proof reading the final draft.

"God will make a way" by Don Moen, Integrity Music©

This book is dedicated with love to my son and daughter

SUSTAINED THROUGH THE TRIALS

INTRODUCTION

This is the true story of how God drew me to His heart following the miraculous healing of angina and how He has been with me through some of the darkest and loneliest times which ensued. The thought of writing a book seemed far-fetched but after several prompts to do so by those with whom I shared my testimony, I finally got started although re-living the pain did not come without a price. It was nerve-racking and many times I attempted to "throw in the towel"; but the grace of God inspired me to persevere.

We all face many situations throughout our lifetime and some of these situations may have the potential to cause intense suffering. Abuse of any kind, whether physical, verbal, emotional, sexual or spiritual can cause very deep and indelible wounding of the heart and mind. This trauma, which can have both an inward and an outward effect, can last a lifetime; however, it depends very much on how we choose to deal with the pain as to the kind of person we become. I chose the 'God intended' way and found that I began to develop a forgiving and compassionate heart towards those who intentionally or unintentionally caused me unnecessary pain and suffering.

However, we are all unique and what may cause profound devastation in one person may simply 'bubble' over the surface of another. I suffered one blow after another; felt crushed time after time and often wondered where was God in all of it. It is not my intention to detail every stressful encounter and as a result I have merely skimmed the surface of what I suffered. I have withheld or changed the names of some persons involved in order to protect their identity and in cases where permission has been granted I have used original names.

The two main objectives of this book are to glorify my Lord and Saviour Jesus Christ and secondly, to encourage readers who are faced with situations similar to those I experienced that there is hope beyond the pain. In writing this book, I have been able to put the pain of my past behind me as too often the pain has held me back from moving on. However, with reference to Corrie ten Boom in her book "The Hiding Place", she states in the preface, "This is what the past is for! Every experience God gives us, every person He puts in our lives is the perfect preparation for the future that only He can see".

1. THE DIAGNOSIS

It was in the month of August 1983 when I was diagnosed with angina which is pain in the chest due to over-exertion when the heart is diseased. This pain can radiate upwards to the lower jaw and down both arms although the pain in the left arm can be more apparent. My son Josh, was four and a half and my daughter Vikki, was six months of age. I was working full-time as a paediatric ward sister and state finalist examiner at a hospital in London having returned to work when Josh was seven weeks old and Vikki was eleven weeks old respectively.

On the evening of the late shift, a colleague noticed that I was in pain and suggested that I be seen in the casualty department of the hospital. The previous evening I had walked very quickly across a pedestrian crossing and noted a heaviness and dull ache in my left arm immediately after crossing to the other side. This discomfort persisted throughout the night making my sleep very disturbed but despite this I went in on the late shift.

Eventually and with lots of persuasion, I reported to the casualty department where an electro-cardiogram was performed. The trace showed changes which led to a range of further tests which were performed over the next eight months. I can clearly recall the doctor giving me the results of the stress test which was done the following day. He said that the findings were as that of a sixty-year-old who had heart disease and only had a few years to live. I was thirty-five. I was shaken and anxious and immediately rang my husband Karl to tell him the news. He was not perturbed in any way and said that it was all in my mind. Our three-bedroom semi-detached home had just been sold so that Karl could invest in a self- employed business and we were in the process of packing up and getting ready to leave. Being told that I should not lift or push heavy objects and to commence regular medication, my doctor was not pleased when I told him that I was in the throes of moving house.

My mother resided in the West Indies and I eventually told her of my medical problems. She suggested that I bring the children from the UK to live with her until we settled in our new home but our 'new home' was a disused cinema for which Karl had recently obtained the leasehold. The building was derelict, gutted, very damp, filthy dirty, had an awful stench, dead pigeons scattered around, live pigeons flying over-head; there was no supply of gas, electricity or water to the building. Everywhere was dark and damp with narrow corridors and small box rooms apart from what was once used as the projector room and the cinema room. Basically, the building was a shell and because the roofing was so bad, the water poured through the many damaged areas when it rained. It was the coldest winter of the century.

Karl had the water and electric supply reconnected to the building and the builders began the work of renovation four months before we sold our house. My mother paid the airfares for the children as a one-way fare and a return fare for me. Eleven years prior, I suffered a slipped disc and the strain on my back from all that is involved with moving house aggravated the backache and sciatica that often affected me. I had to use a wheelchair for travelling despite knowing that this would upset my mother from whom I had managed to shield most of my problems. I had mixed emotions about going to the West Indies because of the added burden of knowing that I would be leaving my children behind and returning to the UK on my own.

On my return, Karl and I moved all our belongings into the gutted building and stored everything apart from the bare necessities in a corner on the ground floor amongst the rubble, dead pigeons and builders' equipment. We used what had been a storage room on the first floor to house the three mattresses, one on top of the other in order to have somewhere to sleep. Karl attached a light bulb at the end of a cable which was hung over a nail on the wall in the room and we had an electric heater which kept us comfortably warm when using the room. All night long, pigeons sitting on the ledge of the outer wall of the room made irritating noises. Most nights Karl would leave me alone in the building and return in the early hours of the morning. I found this quite frightening and would stay awake until he returned. I got into the habit of sleeping for one to three hours every night. If I complained, it would only lead to a confrontation which exacerbated attacks of angina. There was one functioning toilet that he located but we could not have a bath or shower because there was no hot water or gas supply to the building, neither was there a shower unit nor bathtub. Well, normally there wouldn't be a bathtub or shower unit in a cinema. So, until many months later when a shower unit was installed and the gas supply was connected, we continued to have a daily bath at the home of a relative of Karl's. On the top floor in the room that he envisaged would be our kitchen, we placed a microwave oven on a table. There was a sink with access to cold water only and there was no connecting drainage pipe. A bucket which had to be emptied several times during the day, was placed under the outlet of the sink to catch any water whenever we opened the tap to wash our hands or the dishes.

2. NO DESTINATION IN SIGHT

After eight months of living in this manner and with very little communication between Karl and me, I felt near to breaking point and took up an offer his cousin made for me to stay with her and her three children in their three-bedroom house. It seemed more feasible than living in a place that was unfit for human habitation and we agreed on a reasonable rent. I shared a bedroom with her two younger children and for a short time she minded her friend's baby who also shared the room with the three of us. I slept on the top of the bunk bed which was not very easy to climb into because of my back problems. I was greatly stressed; working full-time in a very demanding job, suffering from angina and backache, not living in my own home, very little respect from the children, very little privacy and very little sleep at nights owing to a crying baby or the head-banging of the youngest daughter who slept on the lower bunk. With no central heating in the house I was uncomfortably cold. The discomfort was further exacerbated because I was forced to remain indoors not having been offered a set of keys to the house. This made it difficult for me to leave the house when everyone was out for fear of not being able to get back in when I would have needed to.

Three months later I decided that I had to leave. As I was packing my belongings I had a telephone call from my mother in the West Indies. She said that she was just dozing off for an afternoon rest when she heard what sounded like my voice calling out to her and she felt she had to ring me to see if I was okay. I told her how distraught I was and that I would no longer be contactable at this address from tomorrow. At half past six the following morning, I left the house with no particular destination in mind, got onto a bus and travelled to the local town centre. It was a cold, grey, cloudy morning. Clad in my winter coat and with a few pounds in my handbag, I walked aimlessly while waiting for the shops to open so that I could buy myself a hot drink and some toast. Later, I rang my brother and asked him if I could stay with him and his family for the weekend. When he said he would have to ask my sister-in-law who was not at home at the time, I felt a sense of disappointment. I was hoping that he might have understood how stressed I was and suggested that I come over immediately. I decided to ring Sheila, whom I had only recently met. I explained my dilemma and asked her if I could spend the weekend with her. She did not hesitate to answer in the affirmative but said that she had sold her house, was moving out the following day and that I could sleep the night on her sofa.

I returned to Karl's cousin's home to pick up my suitcase which I had left in the hallway and rang for a minicab. I sat in the front passenger seat of the cab and just as we drove away from the house, I spotted Karl driving towards us in the opposite direction. He also saw me and knowing his possessive attitude towards me, he displayed the jealousy that I had well known, did a U-turn and began to follow us. When I mentioned this to the cab driver, he said, "Shall I lose him?" I said, "Yes" and he sped off. Karl remained in hot pursuit and eventually arrived at the house where I thought I would be spending the night but Sheila had already asked one of her friends who lived on her own in a three bedroom house in Acton, if she could take on a tenant. After Karl left and having realised that I was not eloping with another man, this other woman whom I did not know came to fetch me and take me to her home which was very close to where I worked.

I continued to work full-time and travelled to and from work by public transport. I was not keen on walking from the train station through the dark alley way to the house when I finished work on the late shift; so I decided to ask Karl to allow me to use the car which was not being used during the day while he worked on renovating the building. He had no idea where I was living until I made contact with him. Following this contact, he asked me to come back. I returned to the building to continue living in the manner from which I had previously escaped. Karl is very strong willed and if he puts his mind to something, nothing could sway him. This always made it difficult for him to even consider my opinion in most matters. Sometimes I just needed reassurance that even though I could not see the end of the tunnel, he could assure me that what he was doing was feasible and in our best interest. Sadly, he never appeared to have the time to listen to my feelings and the quarrels started up again.

I felt I needed help but did not know what to do or where to go. I recalled there was a social services office a few minutes walk away from the building and decided to run away during one very heated argument. I ran towards the office and he chased me. I could not believe that this was what my life had come to. As I approached the front door of the office, he caught up with me and demanded that I return with him. I refused and with both hands, I held on to a nearby lamppost hoping that someone would come to my rescue. No one did. He peeled my hands off the lamppost and frog marched me back to the building.

3. SHOCK AND HORROR

I missed the children very much. My desire was to have six or seven children. However, I was fortunate and very blessed to have two live births out of eight pregnancies. The children were very precious and remain precious to me. One of the very traumatic experiences happened when I was thirteen weeks pregnant. I had worked ten consecutive shifts and was really looking forward to my four days off before my next spate of ten consecutive working days. It was still quite dark at about five thirty in the morning when I realized that I was leaking amniotic fluid. I was a qualified midwife and knew that this was not a good sign and alerted Karl. A telephone call to my doctor's surgery, which was closed, gave us an emergency number which led to an on-call doctor coming out to assess my condition. She immediately rang for an ambulance and before long I was an in-patient at the local hospital.

I was given a side room and put on strict bed rest; in other words, I was not allowed to get out of bed to use the bathroom facilities and had daily washes in bed. Every day the baby's heartbeat was located and heard; however, on the fourth day, I was taken down to the scanning department for a scan but was not told the results neither did I ask for fear of being told what I did not want to hear. The following morning, owing to the fact that I was allowed out of bed the day before, I asked the nurse who was allocated to look after me, if I could wash myself (there was a wash basin in the room). She responded in the affirmative. I sat up and as I stood at the side of the bed to reach for the towel on the towel rail beside the washbasin, I felt a sensation of more fluid being lost. On checking the sanitary towel, I saw the baby's head. In shock and with a sudden yell as I parted my legs, the baby fell onto the floor. A nurse who was walking past my room, heard my scream and came in. I was still in shock as she gave me a clean sanitary towel and advised me to sit down. She then used the bath towel to pick up the baby which she intended to throw away. I hate being a bother but somehow managed to quietly ask if I could see it. She reluctantly allowed me to hold the little baby boy. At thirteen weeks, he was fully formed. I stroked his little body; his tiny fingers, his toes, his ankles. He looked perfect but was not breathing. That was the last time I saw my baby. I have no memorabilia, had no counselling and no one to whom I could talk. Karl fetched me from the hospital when I was fit for discharge, took me home where he left me on my own with Josh who was eighteen months old.

The other babies I lost were when I was about six to eight weeks pregnant when I would begin to haemorrhage. However, on one of those occasions when I was six weeks pregnant, Josh who was six years of age had just arrived home from school and I asked him to post my booking form for me. There was a post box opposite to where we lived and I could look at him as he crossed the pedestrian crossing. He was au fait with the Green Cross Code and we had crossed this crossing several times but for whatever reason, he ran along the pavement and onto the crossing without looking left or right and was knocked over by a car. I had already lost two babies before him. In the early stages of being pregnant with him, I had been in contact with German measles and was only given the all clear by the Obstetrician to continue the pregnancy when I was seven months pregnant. The thought that he could have been fatally injured still haunts me as I clearly remember him in the grey duffle coat lying on the ground. In shock and horror, I ran from the second floor hysterically calling out to Karl. By the time I got to Josh, a passer-by had taken him from the road and was comforting him on the pavement. Someone had already called for an ambulance and soon we were at the local hospital. All examinations and x-rays proved that apart from a grazed ankle, there was no other external or internal injury and he was discharged. That night just as I was about to have a shower, I had a massive haemorrhage and had to be rushed to hospital. It was another devastating experience. I lost the baby.

Once a week I would ring my mother and always spoke to Josh who often cried and said he wanted to come back to be with his dad and me. We had a strong bond and it was evident that he was deprived of the attention and love that I gave him. Vikki no longer recognised me as her mother and accepted my mother as hers. As it was so upsetting for Josh and for me to hear him crying over the telephone, my mother decided to send him back with a friend of a friend of hers. He had spent a total of six months with my mother and after ten months, in the month of October of that year, my daughter was also brought back with my mother accompanying her. The children were now six and two respectively.

We, that is, my mother, Josh, Vikki and I slept on the second floor of the building in a makeshift bedroom which housed a double bed and a bunk bed. Karl slept apart from us on the first floor in another makeshift bedroom. We were not on speaking terms and spoke mainly through my mother and the children. I had never disclosed the marital problems I was having to my mother. She was not aware of the intensity of the domestic violence, the financial problems and other marital problems although I suspected that she became wise to the facts when she visited us and assumed that I was "putting on" a brave face despite the embarrassment and stress I was going through. Two months after my mother brought Vikki back to the UK, she returned to the West Indies.

4. THE REUNION

It was wonderful having the children back home but the tension grew worse between Karl and me. One day in April, six months after Vikki returned from the West Indies and following a quarrel, Karl went out. I took the opportunity to grab my handbag which had five pounds and some loose change in it. In another bag, I packed a bar of toilet soap, toothbrushes and toothpaste, some underwear for the children and me and I went with the two children to the local Council. I was almost totally ignorant of what to do and where to go but I knew that I had to get away from Karl or I would die at his hands. This was not an uncommon threat from him during a quarrel. I arrived at the Council at ten thirty that morning and at five thirty that evening I was given the address of a hostel to which we should go. It was dark and although I had a fear of being out in the dark and had no idea where the hostel was situated, I would have chosen to continue on the journey rather than go back to my Karl. The children were always well behaved but during this ordeal, they were amazing. They never cried or misbehaved or got into a tantrum.

When I got onto the bus, I asked the bus driver if he could inform me when I had arrived at the appropriate bus stop in relation to the road where the hostel was located. A female passenger overheard my conversation with the driver and offered to take me to the hostel because she said she was getting off at the same bus stop and heading towards the same direction. I felt timid and frightened as we walked across the Common towards the hostel in Shepherd's Bush. Curiosity got the better of her and she wanted to know why was I going to the hostel. Without much detail, I told her that I had had enough of what my husband had put me through. She rang the doorbell when we arrived and waited until someone let us in. As she was about to leave she extended her hand to me and I assumed that she was about to shake my hand; instead, she placed a five-pound note in my hand. She never told me her name and I have never had any further contact with this woman.

I had never had the experience of living in a Bed and Breakfast hostel nor did I know of anyone living under such circumstances from whom I could have had some insight. Although the Council officer told me that we would have a double bedroom with a double bed, we were offered a single room with a single bed in the attic. The bathroom was two floors down and the dining room another two floors down in the basement. The room was bare apart from the bed with sheets that did not fit, a chest of drawers, a hand basin and a very small radiator. I showered the children one at a time and carried them in my arms up the stairs and put them on the bed so that they would not get their feet soiled. My father never allowed me to walk barefooted and I grew to hate the feeling of dust or dirt on my feet and treated the children likewise. They had strict instructions not to get off the bed nor open the door while I was having my shower. Despite all that I was going through, I always managed to maintain a sense of order, keeping everything around me clean and tidy.

It was a long day and I was very tired. Josh slept nearest the wall, Vikki slept in between Josh and me and I slept at the end. We had to sleep like planks of wood because the bed was too small for the three of us; if I turned I would have fallen onto the floor. When we arrived, I was told that breakfast would be served at eight every morning. Having had some rest during the night, I woke up the children and we got ready to go downstairs to have our breakfast then spent the rest of the day walking around the Common. We had a MacDonald's meal before returning to the hostel where we went through the routine of showering. The following morning we went down to have our breakfast but were told that we had missed it. "It is only eight o'clock," I said; but unfortunately the clocks went forward that night. We did not have a television set or a radio in the room and no one reminded us that the clocks were to go forward. We were not offered anything to eat; however, with the five-pound note given to me by the stranger on the bus, I was able to afford something feasible for the children and me to eat. We spent the rest of the day walking around the Common until early evening when it was time to go back to the hostel.

On Monday, which was our third day at the hostel, I was advised to report to the local Council where I was given a cheque for a small amount of money to help with buying our meals and the bare necessities. We were now into our fourth day at the hostel and although I hand-washed all our underwear every night, we had been wearing the same outer clothes every day. At six thirty a.m. and clad in my long winter coat and my boots and wearing nothing under the coat, I made the spontaneous decision to take all our clothes to the laundrette. I left the children in the room advising them not to open the door to anyone. The stress of all that I was going through and the stress of trying to maintain my standards of order and hygiene, made me totally oblivious to the implications and consequences of leaving the children on their own in the room. I washed and dried all the clothes and hurried back to the hostel where the children were lying on the bed waiting for me. I dressed them and we were just in time for breakfast.

Later that day, I rang a friend and asked her to contact Karl. I told her to ask him to give her some clothes for the children and certain items that we needed. He refused, telling her that unless he was told where we were staying, he would not send the things I requested. In fact, he wanted to come over to the hostel. I agreed to this but as he was not allowed entry to the building, I took the children down to the car that was parked nearby. He cried when he saw the children and begged me to go back home with him. He promised to change his attitude towards me and at that point, I relented and the following day he came and took us back with him.

In some small way, it was good to be back where we lived. Josh who had missed school for the past week because of the distance, was now able to continue his education. The second floor was now cleared of all rubble and although all the walls and flooring were bare concrete which required plastering, the rooms could be easily identified as two bedrooms, a sitting room, a dining room and a kitchen. A shower unit and toilet facilities were installed. There was dust and sand everywhere and I spent a lot of time cleaning and keeping the area as clean as was possible. We put the beds, the dining table and chairs and sitting room suite in their respective positions. Karl's decision was to concentrate on getting the business started before commencing any decorating to the second floor where we hoped to make our home. We spent almost two years with bare walls and no carpets apart from a large rug in the sitting room on which the children played with their toys. Fortunately, they always got on well with each other and they both enjoyed drawing; once they had pencils and paper they would be so quiet, one would not believe that children were around.

5. LONGING FOR A FATHER'S LOVE

It was about midday one day when I had a telephone call from my mother who told me that my father was in the UK and he was staying at the home of a couple, friends of mine, to whom I had introduced him during a previous visit. I rang him immediately after speaking to my mother. We spoke at length and at the end of our delightful conversation, he suggested that I ring him the following day.

I was excited not just to speak with him but also to see him and decided to give him a surprise. My father has always had a fascination for aeroplanes and I knew he would love to go for a drive to Heathrow Airport and look at the planes landing and taking off. He was always particular about the way he dressed, making sure that the colours contrasted nicely; tie, socks and the handkerchief which was placed in the top outer pocket of his jacket all matched. I decided that I wanted the children and me to look our best to impress him. I guess I was still trying to please him. Josh looked a perfect little gentleman in his white jacket, dark shirt and trousers and a white bowtie. Vikki looked like a princess in a pretty pink and white flared dress and I thought that I did not look too bad myself.

As I drove over to see my unsuspecting father, I told the children that Dad, as they also called him, would go with us to see the planes. I felt confident and excited. I parked outside the house and using the car phone, I rang my father. I noticed a change in the tone of his voice which was very different from the previous day, when I said, "Surprise, surprise, I am outside of the house." He immediately said that he did not want us to come in and that he would come out to meet us. He came out to where we were waiting on the pavement outside the house. I wanted to hug him. It was many years since I had last seen him and despite the manner in which he treated me, my mother always said, "He is your father; love him." I wanted him to tell me that we looked lovely; that he was happy to see us and that he was proud of us.

Instead, he cold-heartedly told me that he no longer wanted to have anything to do with my mother, my two brothers and me. "What have I done wrong," I timidly asked. I felt as if I were in a dream. Could this really be what I was hearing? I tried to remain composed but I began to feel faint. In a whisper and feeling choked, I said, "We had such a lovely conversation yesterday, what has changed?" He told me that he had nothing against me, that I had done no wrong but that he no longer wanted to have anything to do with my mother, brothers and me.

I swallowed hard to withhold the tears. I had by now, learned the art of remaining stoic in stressful situations but my strength was waning. I felt rejected by Karl and now by my father; the pain was indescribable. The children, I think, were oblivious to the conversation as Vikki played hopscotch on the pavement and Josh looked on at her. I suggested that we go for a drive to the airport in the hope that we would be able to talk further and he would be able to rethink all that he had said but he refused and went back to the house.

The children and I got back into the car. I felt weak and nauseated. I could have died. I really struggled to hold back the tears. After all the years of living in the hope that one day he would be pleased with me and show me his love, I could not believe that he was rejecting me so cold-heartedly and so openly for no apparent reason. Josh who was in the back seat with Vikki asked, "Why isn't Dad coming to the airport with us?" The children addressed my mother and father as 'mum' and 'dad' respectively. I had to be strong for my children and tried to remain cheerful but I was broken. My heart actually felt broken. I told Josh that dad could not go with us today and that we would go another time. I drove back to our home very, very slowly. Karl who thought we were going to the airport asked why had we returned so soon. I told him that it was inconvenient for my father.

The following day I rang my mother and told her what happened. She said that my father was visiting the UK with his secretary. Apparently he began having an affair with his secretary during the time my mother was in the UK having a coronary by-pass operation. It was no wonder that he did not want me to be aware of his relationship with a woman many years my junior.

6. THE SHY PERFECTIONIST

I was born into the Anglican faith and believed in God but did not belong to a Church for the first seventeen years I had been a resident in the UK. However, I regularly prayed at nights before going to bed. I would say the Lord's Prayer and a few other prayers I had learnt by heart from the Anglican Common Prayer Book. Karl was a Catholic but likewise did not belong to a Church. Apart from a brother who lived in the UK and who appeared not to be concerned with my agonising situation, I had no family to off load the silent burden that weighed me down. Financial problems made it difficult for me to ring my mother as I would have liked and my domestic situation hindered me from making new friends or keeping the friends I had before I was married. There was no one at work I could trust enough as a confidant. I felt very isolated.

I grew up with a father who was very strict, demonstrated no apparent love for me and would not hesitate to use the belt or whatever he could lay his hand on to chastise us, that is, my two brothers and myself. Even when he was not angry and appeared to be playful, he seemed to take a delight in inflicting pain on me. I feared for my mother who had heart problems and also suffered physical and verbal abuse from him. She worked full-time as a confidential secretary and was often regarded as a 'gentle lady'. As a child, I do not recall her ever giving me a real hug or saying she loved me. She was always there for me but seemed distant, probably because she was so taken up by the problems she had with my dad. I grew up being afraid of just about everything – my father, anyone in authority, afraid of getting things wrong, the dark, the servant and my school friend's father who sexually abused me, death, – everything. As a result, I became very insecure and grew to be a coward.

My dad's attitude towards me turned me into a

perfectionist. I wanted him to love me and tried to please him in every way that was possible but he persistently ridiculed me about my shape and other aspects of my body in front of our family and friends. It came as no surprise that members of my family emulated his ridicule. He often referred to me as a vine because I was very thin and tall and as a school colleague once described me, "without ship shape or Bristol fashion." He once said in response to his friend's comment that I was a lovely child, that I was more deaf and dumb than his friend's niece who was truly deaf and dumb. I became very shy, lacking in confidence and self-esteem yet always trying to please. I was forced to develop the art of remaining composed and non-complaining or weeping whether I was punished at school, sexually abused or bullied. In a way, it was always easier to be the victim and smile through the pain whether physical or emotional. One day at school, I recall looking over my shoulder at one of the pupils who was being beaten with a rod across his buttocks. In a flash, I too, was given six lashes with the rod for taking a quick glance. With little protection from my school skirt and my thin frame, I felt the searing pain throughout my body and could not sit properly on the chair because my back was so sore. I wanted to cry but dare not because my father was due to pick me up from school and this was the last lesson.

I was still feeling the awful stinging pain in my body when I could see my father at the school gate. I walked slowly towards him hoping that my countenance would not reveal any sign of pain but he did notice something and asked what was wrong and had I been crying. I told him that I was okay but that the very bright light from the sun was causing my eyes to water and squint. If my father realized that I had lied to him, only God knows what further pain I would have gone through.

7. HEALED OF ANGINA

While still being treated for angina I showed no outward emotion and subdued the agony that I could die of a heart attack while my children were quite young. I would often pray after I had settled them for bed then retire to the makeshift sitting room which had the awful stench of damp newly plastered walls. Although I was tired, I was afraid to go to sleep in case I would die in my sleep. Often I would go to the bedroom and gaze at the children while they slept. I would admire their beautiful faces, hold their fingers and stroke their hair, while thinking of how much I loved them. One night while sitting on the sofa which we had positioned in what eventually became our sitting-room, I said, " Dear God, please take this angina away from me" and eventually went off to bed.

I continued to work full-time as a ward sister and looked after the children when I was not at work. The cleaning was endless. Owing to the badly damaged roof which allowed rain to seep through, the ceiling had large patches of mould. After hours of cleaning the mould day after day with bleach, I would develop laryngitis every week. This lasted about four to five days with treatment. I have a propensity to be meticulous and this made it easier for me to keep a sense of order. It was tedious trying to keep the children from leaning on the newly plastered walls which left white marks on their clothes and still allow them to relax and enjoy their moments of play. With all the heavy work I did from day to day, I was always in a lot of pain in my lower back and down my legs especially at the end of the day. Karl showed no compassion towards my condition. To the outsider, life appeared to be normal but deep within me I longed for someone to talk to. I knew that the manner in which Karl treated me was not right. Whenever we had an argument, which was very frequent, he often told me that I was mad or that one day he would kill me. I fell into the trap of believing that I was mad and one day following an argument went to my GP in a very distressed state. As he began to write out a prescription for Lithium, I interrupted him and told him that if I had had those tablets the day before I might have used them all at once. At that point he asked me what I wanted. When I told him that my husband keeps telling me that I am mad, he said he would refer me to a psychiatrist.

A few days later I collected the referral letter and eventually had an appointment to see the psychiatrist. In the presence of a community nurse he questioned me about my circumstances dating back from when my parents were born to the present. At the end of the session, he said that he was employed to treat the mentally ill and that he could not find any sign of mental illness in me. He went on to say that he was surprised though, that living under those circumstances, I had not had a mental breakdown. There was nothing he could do for me. The nurse who was present, said that she could relate to what I was going through and would be happy to see me on a weekly basis. This I did until she felt I no longer needed to see her.

I was still working full-time when one day, I left my office and headed to the ward only to be met by a woman who said she had been visiting the patients. She had done this before but this was the first time I had seen her. She said she was the assistant to the hospital Chaplain who was away on holiday and she was filling in for him. My heart leapt. Without hesitation I invited her back to my office and told her I needed to talk about a problem that was a big burden for me. It was already eight months since I was diagnosed with angina. Sylvia seemed to have all the time in the world for me and allowed me to pour out all my innermost feelings. The emotional pain already seemed halved as I spoke at length. She then asked me if I would like her to pray for me. I could not say 'yes' more quickly. After she prayed she invited me to the church to which she belonged. She normally took the evening service on the first Sunday of every month.

Karl was very controlling not unlike my father. He

made it very difficult for me to go out on my own other than to work and it was easier to give in to him to avoid conflict. However, he did not object when I asked him if I could use the car to go to the service. It was raining and the petrol gauge on the car was on empty. Putting in five pounds worth of petrol did not shift the gauge much but taking Josh with me and not knowing exactly where the church was, I drove in the direction Sylvia gave me stopping twice to ask for directions. I was late arriving for the service and missed almost all the sermon. I spotted Sylvia and decided to sit next to her. Within a few minutes, the guest speaker ended his sermon and asked if there was anyone who wanted prayer. I noted that a few people had raised their hands. With a problem that I wanted to be rid of, I raised my hand only to withdraw it immediately not knowing what I was letting myself in for; but he spotted me and pointing to me asked me to come forward. I was nervous and not keen to comply but Sylvia, offering to accompany me, suggested that I go up for prayer.

The speaker asked me what it is that I wanted prayer for. I told him and he proceeded to call out the names of a few people, I think three, from the front who were asked by him to support him in praying for me. It was over in a few minutes. I saw no flashing lights and nothing untoward took place. I hurried back to my seat next to Josh while other people went up for prayer. I told Sylvia that I had to get back home because I had told Karl that I would be back at eight pm and it was already seven forty-five.

During my shift on the Friday, two days before that Sunday, I had had a telephone call from the hospital telling me that a bed was booked for me to come in on the Tuesday after the Sunday. When I arrived at the hospital, I was told that there were no beds available and that I should return the following day. This I did and being first on the list, I immediately had to change into my theatre gown on arrival. Everything was done hurriedly - all the notes and the usual checks such as blood pressure, temperature and signing of the consent form. Then the theatre assistant came to collect me. As I was being wheeled on the trolley towards the elevator, the ward sister called out to the theatre assistant stating that she had forgotten to pre-medicate me. Quickly she injected me with a sedative.

It seemed as if it were only a lapse of a few minutes before I was on the theatre table. I had not yet begun to feel any effect from the sedative; I guess the apprehension caused a surge of adrenaline through my blood vessels thus delaying the effect. A huge x-ray machine was placed over me, big enough to almost cover the upper half of my body and close enough to almost touch my nose. I turned my head to the side in order to see the monitor. The surgeon made an incision in my groin and a radio-opaque catheter was inserted into the vein. The surgeon informed me that he would 'flush' my veins and that the solution contained a radio-opaque dye. This procedure was not a very pleasant experience and lasted approximately forty minutes. On the monitor I could see the catheter like that of a very long earthworm crawling up my vein. The solution contained a drug which caused all my blood vessels to dilate so that the coronary arteries could be observed for any blockages. Each of the three flushes made me feel as if every part of my body on the inside was about to explode but fortunately the effect only lasted a few seconds.

At the end of the investigation, the surgeon looked down at me still lying on the theatre table and said, " Well, I can't find anything wrong with your coronary arteries. You should stop taking all the medication and start swimming or playing tennis." I was just beginning to feel drowsy from the pre-medication when the biggest, broadest smile came across my face as I blurted out, "They prayed for me on Sunday; they prayed that God would heal me and He has." The surgeon looked at me with raised eyebrows and handed me over to his assistant who sutured the incised area. It was a lovely feeling as I was being wheeled back to the ward; I was drowsy but smiling as the trolley was manoeuvred through the corridors of the hospital. I kept saying to myself over and over, "God has healed me, He answered the prayers that were said for me."

I was discharged the following day and went back to work a few days later. Sylvia came up to the ward to see how I had got on at the hospital. When I told her that the surgeon could find nothing wrong, she praised God. She asked me to write out my testimony for the church magazine which I did immediately. She also told me that Satan would attack me in various ways to distract me from keeping my eyes on the Lord. I was so filled with a joy that I could not explain; I felt I loved everyone, I was so happy. I could not understand how I could ever take my eyes off the Lord and stop thanking Him. A Christian friend told me that soon I would come down to earth and carry on with the mundane things but this feeling of ecstasy lasted and lasted.

8. THE SEARCH BEGINS

One day Sylvia rang and told me that Steve Ryder, an evangelist, would be speaking at a venue near to where I lived and that I should, if possible, attend the meeting. There was still very little communication between Karl and me. However, when I asked him to allow me to use the car that evening, to my surprise and delight, he did not object. I almost felt guilty going out on my own and especially in the evening but I was so filled with the excitement of finding out more about this God who healed me of angina.

I was the first born of three children and the only girl. My father was over-protective and controlled all of my going out and the friends with whom I played or associated. Apart from school, church, ballet and the occasional visit to family and close friends, I had to stay indoors. I was never allowed out after dark (in Trinidad where I was born, dusk begins around five pm). I became adjusted to a very strict regime and very fearful of my dad. In fact, I grew to be fearful of the dark whether indoors or outdoors and often had to sleep with a light on in the bedroom. Having witnessed my dad beat my brothers in a violent manner, the fear of being beaten meant that I was always keen to please him. I recall him hitting me on my thigh with his hand. We were standing facing each other and I thought he was playing a game with me as he held both my hands in his. As I leaned backwards still holding onto his hands, I pretended to be spider-man (or woman) and lifted one leg to begin to 'walk ' up his legs. He assumed that I had attempted to kick him and in anger he smacked me on my bare thigh. I was wearing a pair of shorts at the time. The stinging pain was enough to make me cry but I withheld the tears. I had learnt by now that crying was not acceptable and as soon as he went out, I ran over to my grandmother who lived opposite. I took a risk because we were not allowed to visit or speak to my maternal grandparents owing to a family dispute which began before I was born. My grandmother, of mixed race (half Chinese and half Indian) and a dear woman, treated me with much affection (in secret), rubbed some oil on the reddened area which soothed the burning. His handprint from the smack lasted for more than a week.

With a husband who was not unlike my father in many ways, I found it easier to comply with his demands. Going out on my own in the evening to return at night was not something I would think of doing but I felt a great desire to go to this meeting which was held at the local town-hall. When I arrived, the large room was already packed although the meeting had not yet begun. The only available seat I could see immediately was one in the front row. Not wanting to be left standing, I walked over quickly to the position and sat down next to a man who eventually introduced himself as Michael. He had his disabled mother in a wheelchair beside him. Shortly after taking the seat, the meeting started and the choir broke out in worship songs. I was not au fait with the songs but there was something very beautiful about them as I quietly read the words on the screen. It wasn't long before I began singing along.

The worship lasted about one hour. There was an exciting buzz in the atmosphere in the hall. After a few messages Steve Ryder took centre stage on the platform. He preached for about forty minutes on Ezekiel chapter 38. At the end of the sermon, he invited people to come forward for prayer to accept Jesus into their lives, for healing, for deliverance and whatever they needed prayer for. Sitting in the front row gave me the opportunity to see all that was happening as people came forward forming a line in front of the stage. The choir carried on with worship songs as Steve came off the platform and walked to one end of the row of people. He would spend a minute or so asking what were their needs and pray with them accordingly. I could hear him saying very loudly, "In the Name of Jesus, be healed" or whatever, in response to the person's needs. Almost everyone he prayed for fell to the floor. I had heard stories of people attending events of a similar nature and being pushed on the forehead to force them to fall. I certainly was not keen to encounter that experience.

I have a propensity to be fussy over standards of hygiene and that day, not only had I shampooed my hair, I was wearing a white top and white trousers, white being my favourite colour. As much as I felt a wonderful sense of excitement at being present at this event, I felt that there was no way I was going to lie on the floor and get my hair and clothes soiled. As a result, I did not go forward; but God is so amazing, He had His own agenda. However, I was still so thrilled at being healed of angina ten months earlier, I really wanted to get to know more about Jesus who had heard my cries and answered the prayers of those who had prayed for me.

Steve came to the end of that line of people, went back on the platform and made a second plea for people to come forward. Somehow I felt he was talking to me. My heart was pounding. Michael looked at me and said, "Let's go." We stood about six feet in front of our seats and joined the line that was being formed. However, as Steve came down the line speaking to and praying for each person, he went past us because it appeared, he thought we were 'catchers'. 'Catchers' are the people who stand at the back of the person being prayed for to catch them as they begin to fall.

Michael and I decided to go back to our seats. Steve went back to the microphone and again announced that there were people present who the Lord was calling and that they should come forward. I could hear people weeping, laughing, praying and singing along with the choir. Michael and I went forward. He was standing on my right as Steve approached from the right. I could hear Steve very loudly saying, "In the Name of Jesus, be healed." As Steve approached the person on the right of Michael, I closed my eyes not knowing what to expect and that was it!! When I opened my eyes, I was lying flat on the floor. How did this happen? Did Steve come face to face with me? Did he speak to me? Did he lay his hands on me? Did I fall before he came near to me? I turned my head to the right only to see Michael just about to get up from the floor.

I began to laugh and cry at the same time. For many years through pain and suffering I would often withhold the tears but this felt so good. I felt such a wonderful release and joy as the tears cascaded down my face without effort. Michael offered his hand to help me to my feet. This was truly amazing. I felt so happy. I was oblivious to any 'dirt' that might have got on my hair or clothes and really, I was not bothered. As I stood to my feet, I realized that my body had no feeling of weight. I could not feel my feet touching the floor and a strange feeling that I might fall over if I tried to walk unaided.

We were laughing, crying and praising God as Michael helped me back to my seat. When I felt able to talk, I asked Michael if he saw what had happened to me. Did Steve speak to me? Did I speak to him? How did I arrive at lying on the floor? He was on the floor before Steve approached me and was unaware of what happened. I noted that some people fell in a manner that looked as if their bodies jerked, their hands moved upwards, their knees bent as they would fall to the floor. My feeling was that angels lifted me and gently laid me on 'Holy Ground' – clean, pure, holy ground. I felt nothing nor heard anything as I lay on the floor not that the prayers and praising had stopped. I really believe the Lord Jesus Christ momentarily took me "beside the still waters" (Psalm 23 Verse 2), and filled me with His Holy Spirit. The peace I felt was tangible.

The meeting came to a close and I was very conscious of the walk back to the car in the dark; but I was so full of an inexplicable joy that I became oblivious of walking to the car which was not parked nearby. I clearly remember the wonderful joy I felt as I drove all the way home. My countenance felt radiant as I smiled and sang a beautiful chorus I had learnt that night:

> "He is Lord, He is Lord;
> He is risen from the dead and He is Lord.
> Every knee shall bow, every tongue confess
> that Jesus Christ is Lord."
>
> Anon.

That night Jesus became my personal Lord and Saviour. What I found remarkable was that even before I repented of my sins and asked Jesus to come into my heart and take control of my life, He healed me of angina. When I arrived home I wanted to share all that took place at the meeting with Karl but he was looking at a documentary on the television about Haley's comet and was not interested in anything I had to say. How I wished he would want to know more about the God who created the heavens and the earth and all in them. (Psalm 24 Verse 1).

9. A SPIRITUAL HUNGER

At the meeting, I noted that one of the notices given at the outset of the evening indicated that Steve would be at a forth-coming meeting in a town outside London. I could not afford to miss out on what the Lord had for me. Much to my amazement, when I mentioned this to Karl, he decided to go with the children and me. No one could understand the excitement I felt.

We drove many miles out of London to the meeting which was conducted in the same manner as the one I attended at the local town hall. The four of us went forward at the alter call. There was still tension in our relationship so I felt inhibited to ask Karl if he accepted Jesus as his Lord and Saviour. In a way, it was easier for me to assume that he had than to ask a question which may have led to a quarrel.

A few months later, I was introduced to Kim who eventually became a friend. On her first visit to me (this was a big step for me because Karl indirectly prevented me from having friends), she gave me a Bible. I remember saying, " I will read this from cover to cover." However, after Kim left, I looked at the Bible and thought that I would never have time to read all of this. Much to my surprise, I found that every evening, after I had settled the children to bed, I had a great desire to read the Bible. I began reading the New Testament and started with the Gospel of Matthew. I read about a chapter every night and by the time I got into Romans, I was so filled with awe that I purchased a highlighter pen and began to highlight all the verses where I believe the Lord was speaking directly to me.

I eventually completed the whole of the New Testament and was curious to find out what was in the Old Testament. I therefore continued to read as much as I could before falling asleep. Months went by and although I continued with the same daily chores, everything seemed 'lighter'. Kim and I planned that she would visit me once a week and during this time we did Bible study. She really opened me up to the amazing love of Jesus and taught me much. I was really falling in love with Jesus who suffered and died for me. Kim lent me dozens of Christian audio and videotapes, magazines and books. The more she shared with me, the more 'hungry' I became. This was great; this was so exciting.

It was not long before I found a church. I really believe that if anyone truly seeks the Lord Jesus, He will reveal Himself to him or her. I had an inner desire to go to Church and suddenly recalled a notice given at the Steve Ryder meeting that Steve was going to be at another meeting in the local town centre. I was amazed at the ease with which Karl allowed me to go when I asked him for the car. I took the children with me. We arrived just as the closing worship song was being sung. As we entered the hall, we were facing the backs of the congregation of about four hundred strong, most of them had their hands raised as they sang "Shine Jesus shine" by Graham Kendrick. It was the first time I heard this worship song; it sounded heavenly. This was not just a one off meeting, it was a Church (Church referring to the people rather than a building) that met every Sunday morning and evening and Steve was a guest speaker for that evening service.

It was a miracle that Karl allowed me to use the car most Sunday evenings to go to Church with the children who looked forward to the meetings. However, one Sunday when I could not have the car for the evening service, the children and I went in the morning. I was amazed to find that the morning service was just as exciting as the evening service. When I told Karl that we would like to go to church twice on a Sunday, again to my surprise, he did not object. God was really opening up the pathway for me to grow closer to Him.

God made a way for His people, the Israelites, to escape from Pharaoh by parting the Red Sea and holding up the waters until the Israelites had passed through (Exodus Ch.13). There is a worship song that goes like this,

> "God will make a way where there seems to be no way;
> He works in ways we cannot see,
> He will make a way for me.
> He will be my guide, hold me closely to His side,
> With love and strength for each new day, He will make a way."

I was bursting with joy and excitement of this newly found love that the Lord was revealing to me. I had longed for my father's approval and love; instead, God, my Heavenly Father was showering His love on me. I seemed to become oblivious to all the stress and strain and began to feel a deep compassion towards Karl instead of being afraid of him and the hate I felt for the manner in which he treated me.

I had completed reading the Bible from cover to cover and decided that every night I would have family worship because I wanted to read the Bible, God's Holy Word, to the children to impart the amazing love of God to them. Fortunately, we never had enough money to buy children's storybooks about monsters, ghosts and the like; it would have been a waste of money. I often invited Karl to join the children and me but he always refused. Just before I settled the children for bed we would get together on my bed and having learnt some songs at church, we sang our favourites with my son accompanying us on the guitar. It was really lovely to see how much the children loved the time we spent praising the Lord. They wanted it as much as I did and we placed no time limit on the sessions. After a time of singing, I would read a chapter or part for our Bible reading. I began with the New Testament starting with the Gospel of Matthew. They took turns in reading and following that, we prayed.

Although I was shy of praying out aloud having been

brought up in the High Anglican Church where it was not the done thing, the children and I prayed as the Lord led us. There is something so beautiful listening to the uninhibited, pure and innocent prayers of a child. The children often asked questions about Jesus and other passages as we read the Bible. My fear of not being able to answer their queries was short-lived. I used to pray when alone asking God to reveal the answers to me whenever the children asked me anything about the Bible. I was amazed at God's grace. Every time without fail when I was asked a question, I found myself speaking out a reply that I had not thought of. This was really exciting and I wanted more and much more. I was in a real state of hunger for more of the Lord.

10. GOD'S PROVISION

In 1986 before I gave my life to the Lord Jesus Christ, I resigned from my post as paediatric ward sister for many reasons. The hospital was due to be demolished with a plan to rebuild in five years. Vikki was three years of age. I was under a tremendous amount of stress. The domestic violence continued with Karl and me having fierce fights and on a couple of occasions, the police were called. The financial problems grew worse with the result that bailiffs entered the building when we were out and seized from the business place all they could accumulate to cover the outstanding debt and their costs. I also suffered badly with menstrual problems, backache and sciatica. It was a full-time task to clean the third floor of the building where we eventually made our home. Each time I swept the concreted floor, it yielded enough sand to fill a pedal bin bag. I did this at least twice a day together with cleaning the vast amounts of mould that spread inside the newly built cupboards we had for storing our clothes. I also assisted Karl as he tirelessly worked from about six in the morning to midnight, clearing all the debris from the areas he eventually turned into a self-employed business, caring for the children, coping with all normal house-hold chores and helping the children with their homework. At the ages of seven and three respectively, they were accepted at the same Independent Preparatory School where a higher standard of education and performance were expected of them.

My father, as mentioned earlier, was a perfectionist and at all times everything had to be in order and done meticulously. He always expected a very high standard from me in everything I did which included diction and grammar but he never praised me. I was never able to please him although I grew to be a perfectionist. However, cleaning the area where we lived and keeping a sense of order was a challenge. One night while we were asleep, I thought I could hear our pet cat clawing at the end of the bed. "Stop it," I said; but he persisted. As I leaned forward to dissuade him from the clawing, I felt large drops of water fall onto my head. It was raining and the water was coming through the ceiling, through the ceiling light and onto the bed. Another time when we sat down at the table to eat our dinner, the rainwater began to fall through the ceiling and onto my son's plate. Each time without fail, when it rained, the water came through the building in many places. We eventually had to keep a pile of containers which we would place in all the areas where the water came through the roof.

When Vikki was four years of age, I applied for a job as a medical coder. This was an office job which required an experienced registered nurse to code medical data on the computer. Having been out of work for four years, it was a bit daunting to find a Monday to Friday job in an office and having to use a computer unlike wearing a uniform and working in a hospital. However, there was on the job training for six months. Prior to this post I had never had any experience in using computers.

I began to settle down and enjoy this new challenge. It was also a good feeling to get dressed up and go out to work rather than to be in a tracksuit all day cleaning and making every endeavour to make the derelict building a home. Joy began to fill my heart and one day I felt a burning desire to tithe. No one suggested it to me; I just felt a deep desire to do so. My father did not like us having birthday parties because he did not want us to get into the habit of receiving. As a result I found that it was always easier to give but had a lot of difficulty in receiving. If anyone gave me anything whether it was material or a compliment, I was never able to receive it gracefully. In fact, I would feel awkward and endeavour to find ways of reciprocating. My desire to tithe was my way of thanking God for all the blessings He was pouring out to me. Having always had Karl control the spending, I was not sure how I would tithe without telling him, so I prayed about it. I also felt a deep compassion for him to accept Jesus as his Lord and Saviour because he showed no signs of change following the Steve Ryder meeting that he, the children and I attended previously. I decided to fast and pray for him. Fasting was another big challenge for me. I was always able to eat anything and any amount at any time and remain very slim. However, I chose to do a 24-hour fast once a week on a Sunday and attend the early-morning prayer meeting held by the church every day, Monday to Friday. The meetings started at six o'clock and finished at seven o'clock. I started work at seven fifteen and the journey from the prayer meeting was about five minutes. It was perfect. God's plans are always perfect.

Four months into my job and before the six months were up, my employer told me that they had decided that as my work performance was up to the standard they expected, they wanted to keep me on and offered me a pay rise. And so God continued to provide; I had a second increase in September of that year and in December had a bonus of a month's salary. I was so in love with the Lord and I felt deeply loved by Him. I made up my own love songs to Jesus, sang worship songs all the time and listened to the audiotapes with a Walkman when not at work. Whether I was cleaning, cooking or doing any household chore, I had the Walkman with me hearing the Word of God constantly. I also took my Bible to work with me and spent my lunch break at my desk reading the Scriptures. I continued to highlight all the areas where I felt the Lord was talking to me. God is so good. I did not think I could become more excited but the excitement was growing as fast as I was finding out more about Jesus, my Lord and Saviour who suffered and died for me so that I could have eternal life with Him (John Chapter 3 Verse 16).

11. THE PROPHECY

As a child I was not allowed to ask for anything. My parents provided what they thought I needed; as a result, I felt a little coy asking the Lord for more but owing to the number of times I was not able to go to Church because of the unavailability of the car, I decided to ask the Lord to provide a car for me. From the date of starting my new job in January to August of that year, Karl never used a penny of my income which was most unusual and I was able to save enough for the deposit. This was a miracle. The Gospel of Mark Chapter 11 Verse 24 states, " Therefore I tell you, whatever you ask for in prayer, believe that you have received it, and it will be yours." I placed a deposit on a new car without Karl's consent or knowledge. When it became evident that I was purchasing a car, he was not happy; but the deal had gone through and I would have lost the large deposit had he stopped me.

When I received the telephone call that the car was ready for collection, I took the children with me. Before we drove off, we prayed and thanked God for His provision. We also prayed that the car and all who travelled in her would be kept safe at all times and that the car would be used for God's honour, glory and praise. By now the children and I had learnt a lot of Christian songs and I had purchased a few audiotapes with worship songs. We played these songs endlessly and tirelessly when we were in the car and at home. If while driving, I stopped at a set of traffic lights, Vikki who was seven years of age would wind the window down and shout out "Praise the Lord" to the passengers and or driver of the car adjacent to us. Together with the videos, audiotapes and Christian literature I borrowed from Kim, I felt I was really growing in knowledge of the Lord but not fast enough.

The children and I were still attending church regularly twice on Sunday and never missed a night of family worship. I could hardly wait for the alarm clock to ring in the mornings to get off to the prayer meeting. I also continued to fast and began after the evening meal to the following day's evening meal. All seemed to be going fine until one day as I was serving the evening meal to the children (it was not yet time for me to eat), when the television news began. The report was on an African country where there was drought and famine. The footage showed the reporter standing near to a mother holding her baby; her husband and their son had gone to fetch some water. Before they returned with the water and while the reporter was still commentating, the mother died. My eyes welled up with tears. Normally if I did not eat regularly I would suffer awful pains in my stomach. I could hardly imagine what this dear woman suffered. I found myself fervently praying for the husband and son who would have returned only to find that the woman had passed away.

One morning on my way to the prayer meeting, I was begging the Lord to let it be today that Karl would accept Him as Lord and Saviour of his life. I remember holding the steering wheel in a sort of desperate manner and praying out aloud, "Please Lord, please Lord, let it be today." When I arrived at the hall where we met every morning, a woman from the church whom I did not know but had seen her several times on a Sunday, came up to me and began to utter verses from the Bible over me. No one had ever done this to me so I was in awe of all that she said and could not take it all in. However, I clearly remember her saying, "Do not strive, do not strive; like David, you have a heart after God's own heart and from your belly shall flow rivers of living waters." No one but the Lord could have known that that morning I was striving and pleading with the Lord to save my husband. God is truly amazing.

That night in family worship, the reading from the Bible stated, "No-one can come to Me unless the Father who sent Me draws him" (John Chapter 6 Verse 44). I was so amazed at how God was talking to me directly from His Word. I underlined the verse and dated it. Excitedly I said

"Thank you, Lord. I no longer have to strive but to hand the burden for Karl over to You and continue to love and pray for him." On the following Sunday at the church service when I met the woman who spoke the Bible verses over me, I asked her to write out all that she had said. This she did and to this day I still have the original piece of paper. I asked her what led her to prophesy over me. She said that she was going on a missionary trip with a group from the Church and the Lord told her that she would meet a woman over whom she should prophesy. It so happened that during the services held in the country they visited, she never felt the Lord's leading to any member of the congregation. On her return to the UK, she attended the early-morning prayer meeting. It was the only time I had seen her at these meetings and as I entered the door of the Community hall, she came directly to me and began to speak out words that really left me speechless.

12. ANSWER TO A CHILD'S PRAYER

The children and I continued to have family worship every night and attended church twice on a Sunday now that I had a car of my own. The building was beginning to take the shape of a business place on the ground floor, an office and self-contained bedroom on the first floor and a two-bedroom maisonette, with two bathrooms, sitting room, dining room and kitchen on the second floor. Having lived in squalor for over three years, both Karl and I decided to have all the walls and ceilings of our new home painted white. We even had white carpets throughout apart from the dining room which had wooden flooring and the kitchen which had white tiled flooring. With spot lighting and large mirrors strategically positioned, the flat looked elegant. The fitted kitchen was white with brass fittings and a brass sink.

It was not a good time economically for Karl to launch the opening of his business because the country was in economic decline and heading for a recession. So three years after the launch of the company, when he decided that he wanted to invest in a six-bedroom detached house with in-door heated swimming pool, I was not too keen to support the idea because the company was running at a loss. However, he went ahead with the purchase and it was later that I found out that the property was not in joint names.

Having moved into a new area, I decided to register with a local General Practitioner. She suggested that I have a well woman check which included a cervical smear test. About two weeks later when I rang for the results, the receptionist informed me that the doctor wished to see me. It was convenient for me to attend the appointment later that day. My doctor wasted no time in telling me that the results of the smear test were abnormal and advised me to have a hysterectomy. I did not want her to tell me that cancerous cells were found so I did not ask any questions.

The company for whom I was working at the time, offered the employees a non-contributory health scheme whereby I would have the privilege of private hospital facilities without having to pay anything towards the costs. My GP suggested that I contact a surgeon immediately and book myself in for the operation. It was the fifteenth of December 1990 and she wanted me to have the operation before Christmas. I booked myself in at a private hospital which was approximately five minutes drive away from our home but the earliest appointment was into the New Year. That night as I lay in bed looking at the news on the television, I heard that a thirty-two year old mother had died of cancer of the cervix leaving two very young children. I felt numb.

Josh was now twelve years of age and Vikki four years his junior when my mother came back to the UK on a visit and ended up staying permanently at the house with the children and me. I was admitted to hospital and all went well apart from the post-operative period when I suffered an adverse reaction to the drugs. I lost my sense of taste, smell and feeling and really thought I was going to die. After two days of persistent vomiting and diarrhoea, the drugs were discontinued and slowly I began to recover and was allowed to sit out of bed. I remember standing at my bedside and aiming to walk towards the door of my room. I felt very faint and lethargic. When I mentioned this to the staff, a blood sample was taken to measure my haemoglobin levels. The result was well below the average and although I was eligible for a blood transfusion, the surgeon I was under was not in favour of giving his patients blood transfusions; instead, I was given an oral supplement.

I met three Christians while in the hospital. One of them lent me a book titled "A Divine Revelation Of Hell" by Mary K. Baxter. My blood count (haemoglobin level) was very low and I was being hydrated via an intravenous infusion. I felt weak and did not think I could read more than a page or two at any one time. However, I had only read the first six paragraphs of chapter one when I began to feel an impetus to read on and on. I completed reading the book of approximately two hundred pages in two nights and three days. This incredible testimony gave me a desire to get out of my hospital bed and tell people of the Gospel of Jesus Christ. Of course this was not possible; I had to wait until I was discharged. However, I shared the information with all who visited me and have since then purchased my own copy which I frequently lend out.

Karl spent most of his days and nights on site at the business place. Both children were still attending the Independent school and were doing quite well. It was easy to put on a front and pretend that all was fine but it was evident that the marriage had serious problems. Through my mother I found out that the mortgage was in arrears. We had by now lived at the house for two years. I suggested to Karl that the children should be removed from the independent schools they attended but he refused. It was only a few months later that he had letters from the Headmasters stating that the children would no longer be allowed to return to school until the arrears of the fees were paid off. They never went back to the independent schools; instead, they were accepted in a local state school with the help of the Pastor of my church.

Josh settled into his new environment very quickly but Vikki displayed some tension which I assumed was as a result of not having her brother with her at the same school. She was very close to him and was accustomed to having him around since she started school. When I realised that she was being bullied I felt a surge of anger in me that made me feel very nauseated. I always endeavoured to protect the children from all pain if it were possible because I could not bear the thought of them ever being in pain whether emotional or physical. When Vikki saw my anger at what she had been putting up with, she simply said, "We can pray for her (naming the child who was bullying her) tonight." I felt incredibly humbled by her remark and was not surprised when the bully, who apparently bullied many other children, eventually turned out to be her best friend. God is so good.

13. WARNING

Family worship became second nature to the children and me and we never missed a night of prayer, Bible reading and singing. It was not something I forced upon them; they were just as keen as I was. In fact, Vikki would go through the Bible before we started and set out 'homework' for Josh and me. She would write out about thirty to forty questions and pretend to be a teacher. We were awarded stars if we got the answers correct. If we giggled, we were scolded. By now, they had completed reading the whole of the New Testament and had started in Genesis. This was my second time of reading the Bible from cover to cover and almost everything seemed as new and refreshing as when I first read it. One night when Vikki was reading Genesis Chapter 50, Verse 15 to 21 (we took turns in reading), I became intrigued by verse 21 which states, "… don't be afraid, I will provide for you and your children." I asked her to re-read the verse and when I wondered aloud as to why was the Lord saying this, she told me to underline the verse and put the date next to it. This I did.

I went to work as usual the following day but every now and then I found myself repeating the verse in my head, "… don't be afraid I will provide for you and your children." It seemed so specific in relating to the children and me. I began to wonder what I might become afraid of. I had learnt by now to 'take' everything to the Lord in prayer instead of worrying about it. Although I prayed, somehow I still seemed to carry a subconscious anxiety as to what was going to happen. Then it happened. One morning, after three and a half years of employment and together with seven of my colleagues, I was made redundant. Hardly a day would go by without some mention on the news of people being laid off work. I never dreamed it would happen to me but God had warned me through His Word. He said, "…don't be afraid……." He did not say He may provide, He clearly said He WILL provide. I had to trust Him although it was not easy. We were all given in writing, an estimate of the amount we would receive. My estimate was Two Thousand, Two Hundred pounds.

We had to pack our bags and leave immediately. Two of my colleagues were tearful as they packed their personal belongings into their bags. I felt a sense of peace because I literally took God at His Word and kept repeating silently "... don't be afraid..." We were told that we should report to the job centre and fill in the appropriate forms to gain further employment. This was such a new experience for me. I was very naïve and knew very little about job employment centres or social security. I told Karl the news when I arrived home but he seemed less than interested. He was more keen to get the redundancy payout to help pay off the arrears on the mortgage.

That night when I was having a shower, I called out to Josh to bring a pen and some paper. I told him to write down as I called out some figures. These were the amounts I owed to different companies from whom Karl had borrowed money in my name. When Josh totalled the amount, it was four hundred pounds more than the estimate of redundancy payment given to me in writing. With some anxiety, I said to Josh that we would have to ask God for another four hundred pounds when we say our prayers tonight. As we had now grown accustomed to doing, the three of us got on my bed and we began with singing the worship songs. Then we read the Bible continuing from where we left off the night before. This was followed by saying Psalm 150 which we had now learnt by heart. We chose to say it every night in case we ever forgot to thank and praise God during the day. Then we took turns in praying and we prayed for the extra money I needed to cover my debts.

The following day, I went to the job centre and brought the forms back home with me. As I went through them, I felt loathe to place a tick in the box which would indicate that I was married. It was eighteen months since Karl and I had had any marital relations or even kissed each other; we were basically living separate lives. I therefore sought the advice of a Christian neighbour who was a Barrister. She told me that although I had not had a legal separation from him, I could count us as being separated because of the deprivation of and breakdown in marital relations. I therefore, submitted the form as being separated from him but still living under the same roof.

It may have been about two weeks later when I had a telephone call from a gentleman who said he was calling from the job centre. He said that I was not eligible for work and that I should go to the Post Office in a couple of days and collect an income support book which I can use every week to get help with buying food. I was totally ignorant of the Social Security system. This sounds naïve but the amount of emotional, physical and mental stress I was under kept me focused only on what I needed to concentrate on from day to day. I was weary mentally and physically. It was almost like the Lord took me on a high and this was a let down. But, I still continued to hear silently "… don't be afraid, I will provide for you and your children."

I had always worked full-time and suddenly I was out of work. It almost seemed weird, having the whole day and the house to myself (Karl would take the children to school and not return until he had fetched them from school). I began to relax and spend more time getting to know more about the Lord. It just felt like a long, relaxing much needed holiday. In the twenty years I had known and been married to Karl, we had never been on a holiday. The children and I always spent the time at home although occasionally we went out for a Chinese meal.

Karl spent his nights at the flat on the premises of the business and would come over to the house every morning to meet the children and take them to school. It was a sense of freedom not having to rush around for a change. I filled the days keeping the house tidy, doing the laundry and cooking as I listened to Christian worship songs and sermons. I was in the kitchen one morning, two weeks after I was made redundant, when the post arrived and although I was not expecting it until the end of the month, I received the cheque with the redundancy payout. Karl had been mismanaging my bank account for some time and although I was responsible for my affairs (I was told by the Bank's Head Office), he often forced me to write cheques for him that I knew could not be paid.

When I read the amount on the redundancy cheque it was thirty-one pounds more (yes, MORE) than we had prayed for. Immediately I rang the companies to confirm the outstanding amounts I owed and without hesitation sent off the respective cheques. I was aware that Karl was anticipating the arrival of the redundancy payout and I knew that he would have used all of it to invest in the business. I had suffered the stress of abuse from people from whom he had borrowed money. I experienced the embarrassment and stress of people coming onto the ward where I worked as a ward sister and other places where I worked demanding that I pay them back the money Karl had borrowed from them. I remember telling one woman that I was not responsible for the situation and had no control over it, that my father taught me not to beg, borrow or steal and if I was responsible for what she was going through, I would rather live on bread and water for each meal and pay her back than to be in debt. Romans Chapter 13, Verse 8 states, "Let no debt remain outstanding, except the continuing debt to love one another…"

One month after I was made redundant, Karl came to collect the children for school. He came up to the bedroom where I was making the children's beds and flung a letter at me while articulating abusive words. I opened the envelope and read the contents. I was just coming to terms with the redundancy and could not believe that the house we were living in was due to be repossessed and that we had a week's notice to vacate the property. We had lived at the house for two years and nine months. "How could this happen?" In horror and disbelief, I read and re-read the contents but kept hearing a silent voice saying, "Don't be afraid. Don't be afraid."

14. HOMELESS

I really cannot recall the first twenty-four hours following the devastating news other than sitting on the floor in the corner of one of the sitting rooms probably for hours. However, the day following receipt of the notice of repossession, after the children left for school, I rang a friend who suggested that I go to the Homeless Families Unit in the town centre. It was very difficult for me to accept that this was part of God's plan but He had shown me enough for me to, as it were, 'walk on the water and not look down' (Matthew Chapter 14 Verse 22 - 33).

Anyway, following instructions from my friend and dressed in a smart jacket and skirt, I presented myself at the Homeless Families Unit. I had never been in such a place and had no idea what to expect. The waiting room was filled with a queue of people sitting on chairs and on the floor or standing holding up the pillars of the room. A cloud of smoke hung in the air and there was an awful stench of stale beer amidst the profane language that seemed to spew out of the mouths of those waiting to be seen. It was obvious I stood out like a sore thumb. I took a ticket from the ticket machine and nervously awaited my turn. That was the first of many visits but the last time I dressed in that manner. A friend suggested that it would be more appropriate if I wore a T-shirt, jeans and trainers and looked a bit scruffy when attending my appointments. I was not sure whether she was joking or being real but somehow I felt a little more at ease dressed in that manner when I attended future appointments.

It was well over an hour before I was interviewed. I felt drained and a mixture of emotions - embarrassment, failure, abandonment and timidity as I replied to the many questions I was asked. I reflected on the day I had to have my vaccinations at school. I was five years of age and as my queue approached the nurse, I could see the little flame in which she would sterilize the one needle that was used to inject all the pupils. She must have seen fear written all over my face as I whispered, "Please, don't hurt me." I anticipated that she might have told me off or given me a smack; instead, she gently drew me with her hand to her side and continued to inject those in the queue. I felt so reassured and in a sense, comfortable and never felt the pain I anticipated as she injected me. It was a similar timidity with which I spoke to the assistant. She too, obviously spotted something of my fear and anxiety. She said that my case was urgent and that I would have to bring all the relevant documents to prove my case of homelessness.

Obtaining the documents was tiresome and tedious because the house was in Karl's sole name and the mortgage company would not release any information to me without his permission. He too, was obviously stressed by all the events and as there was still a lot of tension in the marriage, communication was difficult. We had to vacate the property on the eighth of June 1993 and already a few days from the notice had lapsed. The Homeless Families Unit assistant whom I saw at the outset was assigned to me so that she would always see me on each appointment I had at the Unit. She said that to avoid being put out first thing in the morning of the eighth, she would have the children and me taken into the Bed and Breakfast accommodation on the seventh. It was exhausting physically and mentally trying to collate all the information the mortgage company required, going around the supermarkets and other shops collecting boxes, washing and cleaning everything before packing them in the boxes, labelling each box according to whether it was going into storage or into the Bed and Breakfast accommodation with us and still trying to maintain some sense of order. My previous experience in the hostel was very different from this experience. From hour to hour, every step was an experience I had never before encountered or learnt of from someone else's plight.

Every night the children and I continued to have our

family worship. We prayed for God to help us through this devastating time. The children behaved in a manner to be admired. They never questioned anything that was going on, they continued to pray with me every night with such sweet innocence and trust in God that He will provide. We prayed in unity and in one accord and it was reassuring and comforting to me to have their support in prayer.

Josh and Vikki went to school as usual on the day we were to vacate the property. On several occasions I had reminded Karl to pack the clothes he had at the house before the final date. He paid no heed to my advice. Then at eight o'clock the removal vans came, two to begin with, then later, a third. The beautifully kept home we had lived in suddenly was not recognizable. The five men were in and out of the house, loading up the vans; there was such an upheaval; I felt numb. I could have died in the standing position. Karl was not at the house when the vans turned up and only arrived during the afternoon to begin packing his belongings. The men worked tirelessly from approximately eight thirty that morning to about five thirty in the afternoon only stopping to have a cuppa that I offered them occasionally or to go to the toilet. At four o'clock I collected the children from school and after giving them something to eat, I loaded the car with the two suitcases of summer wear and the bare necessities and we headed off to Wealdstone, an area with which I was unfamiliar.

15. EXHAUSTED BUT BLESSED

I was exhausted mentally and physically as Karl drove us to the Bed and Breakfast accommodation. A few months prior to losing our home, Karl sold his BMW 7 series and we decided that he would take over the keep of my Mazda 323 and be responsible for the monthly instalments as I was no longer employed. As we drove from Harrow to Wealdstone, I had no idea what I would encounter. I felt numb and did not have the energy to think or pray. We were greeted at the door by one of the cleaners who answered when I rang the doorbell. She was expecting us and gave me a set of keys for which I had to pay a deposit of Seven Pounds and Fifty Pence. We were ushered to our ground floor room where we left our two suitcases and a couple of boxes prior to being shown the areas we would need to use, such as the kitchen, the fridge and the kitchen sink. I would have to share the fridge, cupboard and sink with the resident whose room was adjacent to mine. While we talked, other residents were butting in asking her questions and using profane language. I shuddered and silently prayed for God's protection. I led a very sheltered life-style and really needed God's protection much more now. Psalm 91, Verse 7 states, "A thousand may fall at your side, ten thousand at your right hand, but it will not come near you." I had to hang on to those words.

From a six-bedroom detached house, three reception rooms and an indoor heated swimming pool to one bedroom was another big challenge. The double bedroom housed a double bed, a bunk bed, a very small built-in wardrobe and a chest of drawers. We were really blessed to have an en-suite bathroom that had a toilet, a very small hand basin and a shower without a showerhead. Not all the rooms were fitted with en-suite bathroom and toilet facilities. I cleaned the bathroom area and floor thoroughly then changed the bed linen for the ones I had taken with me. I cleaned the wardrobe and the chest of drawers before unpacking the suitcases and the boxes. I had nowhere to put the two suitcases other than on the top bunk bed. In the suitcases, I kept underwear and small clothing folded tidily and the rest of the clothing was put in the wardrobe. "Josh could sleep on the lower bunk and Vikki and I on the double bed," I thought. That night we realised that a box clearly labelled "Bed and Breakfast Accommodation" with my son's schoolbooks and all he needed for GCSE preparation was not with us. We were not allowed to get anything out of storage until we left the accommodation. This caused problems for Josh at school because he had no textbooks from which to study and was penalised for not returning his library books on time. This only added to the stress I was already under. However, a letter to the headmaster eventually settled the matter.

The children never complained and seemed to take it all in their stride. I was still holding on silently to "Don't be afraid …" although I really felt nervous and frightened. I was not street-wise and was not used to associating with, never mind living under the same roof as the people with whom I now had to live. With the room as tidy and clean as I was able to have it, the children and I took turns in having a shower before getting ready for bed. My back ached; in fact, every muscle in my body ached and just what I needed (a good massage), the Lord provided. As I stood under the shower, I was pleased that I did not grumble over the lack of the showerhead because the water came down on me in full force giving me a massage all over my neck, shoulders and back. God is amazing. He is so good. He even attends to the smallest of details. As usual, we continued with our routine before we went to sleep; we had our family worship. Josh got out his guitar and we began to sing among other songs, a worship song we had only recently learnt at church, "I'm so glad that Jesus set me free." It seemed apt because although I would not have chosen a place like this to get away from the life I lived with Karl, I was no longer under his domination.

Karl came every morning to pick the children up to

take them to school and would return them after school. Our room was at the front of the building so it was easy to notice when he arrived. At the outset we had our main meal in the communal dining room but I felt I could no longer expose the children to the profane language that was commonly used by most of the residents. As a result, my bed became the dining table for the next seven months. After the children left for school, I would tidy up the bedroom then have a time of prayer and felt led to study the Book of Job.

Job was "blameless and upright; he feared God and shunned evil. He had seven sons and three daughters, and he owned seven thousand sheep, three thousand camels, five hundred yoke of oxen and five hundred donkeys, and had a large number of servants. He was the greatest man among all the people of the East," Job chapter 1, verses 1 – 3. Job lost his children when the house they were in collapsed on them and they died (Job chapter 1, verses 18 and 19). He also lost everything he owned, yet he "...fell to the ground in worship" when he was given the devastating news (Job chapter 1, verse 20). When his wife told him to "Curse God and die!" His reply was, "....shall we accept good from God, and not trouble?" Although he wished he had not been born (Job chapter 3, verse 11), Job never sinned in what he said (Job chapter 2, verse 10).

16. SO LITTLE YET SO MUCH

In the first week and until I got used to the new environment, I spent almost all of the day in the bedroom only going out to the supermarket five minutes walk away to purchase food and toiletries. Left to myself, I am good at managing my finances and although seventy pounds, fifty pence in Income Support was the only money I had each week, I continued to tithe and we had a hot meal every day. The local butcher sold a tray of eight chicken drumsticks for one pound and ninety-nine pence. I had them cut in half, thus having sixteen pieces of chicken of which I made a stew that was served with rice and mushy peas or sweet corn.

I could not bear the thought of Karl not having a proper meal each day so I decided that when he brought the children home from school, I would have a portion prepared for him. This was put out into a small dish so that he could eat it in the car while it was still hot. I did this for seven months. I also fed the residents who frequently loitered around in the kitchen asking what was I cooking for the day. I always got a lot of pleasure from sharing; from cooking for a few people in the hostel to not knowing how many people I would share a meal with that day. On one occasion I cooked enough for my mother who was visiting me, the children, Karl and myself but all the food was consumed by seven of the residents before the children arrived home from school. I had to start cooking all over again. This was exciting. I had lost my entire savings, home, job and the only source of income was Income Support yet I felt I had so much to give. The more I gave, the more I felt the joy of the Lord. God is so amazing.

Karl fetched us every Sunday morning to take us to Church which was admirable of him. He would meet us after the service and take us to my mother's where we had a Sunday roast. My mother was so disappointed with the manner in which he treated me that she was not keen that he should eat with us. However, after telling her that despite what he had put me through, I had forgiven him and could not bear the thought of having him wait in the car until we were ready to leave, she relented and every Sunday the four of us joined my mother for lunch. In all, he would have covered about thirty miles every Sunday. Friends occasionally came over and collected the children and me to take us to their homes for a meal which was always a real blessing for us. I recall one friend giving me some MacDonald's vouchers; this afforded a big treat for the children. It was a delight to look at their faces as they enjoyed something that I was not able to afford.

Before we left the house on the seventh of June to move into the Bed and Breakfast accommodation, I met someone whom I had not met before and told her that we had lost our home and were being housed by the Council. She told me that normally one would be kept in the accommodation for about two weeks but four months had gone by and the summer clothes I had packed for us were not enough to keep us warm. I had only mentioned this to one of the parishioners at Church the following Sunday when she asked how were we getting on and thereafter, we had bags and bags of clothes given to us. I really think the Lord was teaching me to receive and to be humble. I would never dream of wearing someone else's clothes but here I was, more than thankful for anything to keep us warm until we were housed and got our belongings out of storage. I was also told that I should pay a visit to the local charity shops. This too, is something I never did but was amazed at the wonderful bargains I got. Philippians chapter 4, verse 12 states, "I know what it is to be in need, and I know what it is to have plenty. I have learned the secret of being content in any and every situation, whether well fed or hungry, whether living in plenty or in want."

An American family I met at my Church who were temporarily living in the UK, invited us to join their weekly fellowship group which was held on a Friday evening at their home at the American Base. Every week Shelley would drive over to the hostel, pick us up, take us to her home and then drop us back to the hostel after the group meeting. She suggested that I do my laundry at her home and every Monday morning after the children left for school, she would fetch me, take me to her home where I washed and dried my weekly laundry. One day after doing the laundry, she said she had to go to the supermarket and asked me to accompany her. We chatted as we walked up and down the aisles as she put the items into the shopping trolley. I was keeping my eye on the time because I had to get back to the hostel to cook the evening meal for the children. The trolley was full by the time we arrived at the checkout. The bill was paid and we headed towards her car, then to the hostel. As I was getting out of the car, Shelley said that all the groceries she had purchased were for the children and me. I was truly gob-smacked. How could I ever begin to say thank you. I was still struggling with receiving as she saw the look of disbelief on my face. Shelley helped me with lifting all the bags of groceries into the room and left. As she drove off, I heard that still, soft voice saying, "...don't be afraid, I will provide for you and your children." God is truly amazing.

17. A FRIGHTENING ENCOUNTER

It was not long after we moved in, that the woman sharing my kitchen facilities with me moved into the room next to ours. We met in the kitchen and on introducing myself to her I noted that she was wearing a cross on the chain around her neck. In response to my curiosity about the cross, she said that she was Jewish and had accepted Jesus as her Lord and Saviour. She also stated that she had recently been diagnosed with Hepatitis C and only had a few months to live. My heart went out to her and I offered to help her in any way she wished. She asked me to check on her every morning to make sure she was alive but I extended her request by offering to cook her a main meal every day; I was doing this anyway, for the other residents although unplanned. I also served her breakfast cooked by the staff, while she was still in bed.

I told Gillian that the children and I had family worship every night and she was keen to join in with us. She seemed to enjoy the time we shared. The only problem I had was that Gillian chain-smoked and drank heavily (she said this habit was to relieve the pain for which she had no relief when she took pain killing tablets). Soon I began to suffer from headaches and nausea which I eventually put down to passive smoking. When I suggested to her that as a trial, I should stay away from the smoke (which would mean not being in such close contact), she turned real nasty and began to terrorize me. She would wait until I was about to cook the evening meal and open the shared cupboard which was directly above the cooker. She did this several times while smoking as I stood at the cooker attending to the food; she would also leave all her used utensils in the sink which we shared and I was forced to wash them up prior to washing my own dishes. Sharing the same fridge did not help matters. She also began leaving intimidating notes under my door and waking us up in the middle of the night by banging on our door. On two occasions I was forced to call out an ambulance because she collapsed at our door. Whenever her boy friend, who was a very big lad, saw me in the kitchen, he would make a fist with his hand and hit the palm of his other hand with a loud noise at very close range to me. I complained to the Homeless Families Unit but because Gillian had never physically abused me there was nothing they said they could do. I was scared; really scared, but did not let on to the children for fear of them also becoming afraid. I decided to pray about it. Every day after the children left for school, I prayed fervently asking the Lord to bring an end to the torment I was going through. God is so good. Gillian was found to be intentionally homeless and had to leave the hostel about two weeks after the torment began.

There were other scary moments. The smoke alarm sounded almost every night in the middle of the night owing to the residents smoking illicit drugs (I was told). Having learnt the procedure in the unfortunate event of a fire or the sound of alarm bells during my post as a ward sister, I would wake the children and prepare them for evacuation. This caused such an inconvenience and disruption to their sleep. The children also witnessed women fighting each other and Josh had to call the police on one occasion. The area was noted for being rough and there was hardly a night when one would not hear the sirens of the police cars and the ambulance or witness fights in the street. Our room overlooked the road. One evening when Josh failed to return at eight pm, an hour later than expected, following a visit to his friend's home, all negative thoughts entered my mind. I tried to pray but was so overwhelmed by my worst fears I made the decision to report him as missing. One of the residents who accompanied me waited at the bus stop just outside the police station to keep an eye out for Josh. I gave the police officer all the details but before he could put out the APB, Josh alighted from the bus.

But we had times of joy. Not only did we go to Church every Sunday, we also took some of the residents with us;

guys who were involved in all sorts of crime, came with us on two occasions. I also gave a Bible to one of the residents and led a woman in prayer to the Lord. When she left the hostel she made the surprising effort of attending our Church on a few occasions. One resident told me that my name was mentioned in the dining room as the person to whom they could ask any favours and I would comply. It was no surprise when at six thirty one morning, a resident asked for some toothpaste and another asked for a pair of jogging pants because she had packed all her stuff in preparation to leave the hostel and could not find her trousers. Another wanted a bar of soap. Hardly a day went by without one of the residents asking me for something; yet, it was exciting and such a joy to give.

18. WORN AND WEARY

My father did not like us having birthday parties because he did not want people to be inconvenienced by buying gifts for us; as a result, I grew to enjoy giving but had difficulty in receiving. All the items that were borrowed from me were never returned but that was never an issue. The more I gave, the more I seem to have to give and so we also received. The fellowship group paid for the children and me to join them on a holiday to Hayling Island for a Bank holiday weekend. The children were excited as we headed off to the coast on the Thursday evening. It was about ten thirty when we arrived and those who had arrived before we did greeted us with food and a hot drink in the cosy atmosphere of a large tent. I did not ask any questions but I did wonder where I would be sleeping for the night. I thought it was some sort of a joke when I was told that I would be sharing a small tent with Vikki and one other female adult. I had never been near a tent, never mind having it as my 'home' for the next four nights. It was not funny as the children thought, when I had to get on my hands and knees despite a bad back and crawl into the tent. That was the only way I could get in and out of it!!

I did not have a good night's sleep on my first night for many reasons. I always looked forward to a hot shower before going to bed but there was no such luxury. I had to sleep in the clothes I was wearing; the night was very cold and the hard ground added to my discomfort. It was only when discussing the night I had had over breakfast the following morning that I found out that what I thought was the 'mattress' was in fact the sleeping bag. I had slept on top of the sleeping bag and covered up with a blanket. This was one time in my life where I wished I did not fuss over high standards of hygiene. I made every endeavour to encourage the children to be adaptable and flexible as they joined in with the other children and enjoyed the fun; yet, I found myself still trying to keep everything around me clean and tidy.

At least five months had gone by in the hostel and although the leaders of my Church knew that we were homeless, I found it a surprise that neither of the two Pastors asked me how were we coping or even reassured me that they were praying for us. It could have been that they were waiting for me to come to them or they may have thought that my situation was too much to handle. Eventually however, at the end of one service, one of the Pastors approached me and could not believe that I was so filled with joy despite all I related to him. He and his wife decided to pay me a visit at the hostel a couple of days later. I felt no embarrassment as I showed them around the hostel and offered them a light lunch served from my bed which I continued to use as a table. They listened to all that led up to our situation and then my Pastor looked me straight in the eye and said, "God does not like divorce but He does not like the marriage you are in. You must divorce your husband."

At that time, the thought of a divorce never entered my head because every night we prayed that Karl would give his life to the Lord. However, when the idea was suggested to me, I felt a burden lift from me. With all the problems I had encountered in my marriage, it seemed a good idea to be able to start all over again, on my own with the children. Subsequently, when I went to the fellowship group meeting, I told my group leader what the Pastor had said. He immediately got his Bible and read out to me Corinthians chapter 7, verse 13 which states "And if a woman has a husband who is not a believer and he is willing to live with her, she must not divorce him." He went on to say that with all the respect he had for our Pastor, he could not agree with him and that I should not divorce my husband.

My case of homelessness was still under investigation and it appeared that although I reported my homelessness to the local Unit, the papers were handed over to another Borough because of where our house was situated. This meant that I had to be interviewed for a second time and go through all the paper work yet again. I remember sitting in the waiting area until my name was called. I felt intimidated as I was addressed as 'Miss'. There was at this time a lot being said on the news about black, single and unemployed people. Although I fitted this category, I felt far removed from it. I approached the desk feeling weak and worn out and hoped I would have been able to convince the assistant that all I was going through was not deliberate. She never looked at me as she questioned me. Almost in a whisper I tried to tell her through my tears that I was a trained nurse and had worked as a ward sister before getting married but that the marriage failed and that my situation was out of my control. She showed no apparent compassion. At the end of the interview, I turned around facing the others in the waiting room and headed for the exit. I felt embarrassed and more weak and worn than when I went in. Across the road was a telephone kiosk; I went in, pretended to be making a call and cried. "Why Lord, how much longer. When will all of this end?" A few minutes later and more composed, I went back to the hostel to prepare the evening meal for the children on their return from school.

19. DEVASTATED

It was approximately two weeks later when I had a telephone call just after the children left for school; it was from the Homeless Families Unit where I had been recently interviewed. I was given an address to which I had to attend a viewing of a flat with the hope of moving into it temporarily until permanent residence was offered. Shelley offered to take me. The flat was in a house situated on a main road with a pedestrian crossing directly in front of the house. Immediately I thought of the inconvenience of off-loading our possessions a few yards up on the main road and carrying the lot to the flat.

The council officer who met us at the house led us up the staircase to the room we were being offered. I began to feel claustrophobic because there was very little natural light in the hallway and the walls were painted brown. There was a brown wardrobe on the landing and a double bed in the bedroom. I had seen enough. Horror filled my thoughts. "One day here and I would surely have a mental breakdown," I thought. The children would have to change schools again just as they had become settled in their new schools and just as Vikki was no longer being bullied. The flat and the location were not suitable and as a result I refused to take up the offer.

Within a couple of days I had another telephone call informing me that I was being offered permanent housing in a flat in Stonebridge Park Estate. When I mentioned this to the owner of the hostel, she told me that she had come to know the children and me over the past months and from what she had heard of this notorious estate, we would not 'survive' living there. She said the estate was rife with crime, drugs, and prostitution. I broke down and rang Shelley. "Shelley," I cried, "I can't continue like this; I really can't. It's too much." I felt emotionally, physically and mentally drained. Shelley pleaded with me. She said, "God would not bring you this far and abandon you. Hang in there." I rang the Housing officer and when I told her that I could not accept the second offer, she told me that they no longer have a responsibility to house me and that I should leave the hostel immediately. I was devastated. There was no compassion, no understanding. After all, I was only a number in a line of thousands of homeless families. I wondered where was the Lord in all this. I felt abandoned but Hebrews chapter 13, verse 5 states, "Never will I (the Lord) leave you; never will I forsake you". Trusting God during the testing times can be very, very difficult but I had to hold on to His promise, "Don't be afraid, I will provide for you and your children."

I told the owner of the hostel that we had to leave but that we had nowhere to go. She suggested that I rent the room from her and apply for Housing Benefit so that I would not have to be put out, literally on the street. On her instruction, I hurried over to the Benefits Office before the children arrived home from school and waded through the many pages answering the relevant questions on each page. I would not regard myself as unintelligent but I found the filling in of the forms very stressful and almost difficult to understand the questions asked. I handed in the completed forms and hurried back just in time to cook the evening meal.

Throughout my growing up years I had never experienced any hardship of this nature. We had a live-in servant who did all the household chores and more. I never cooked a meal, never did the groceries, laundry or the like. We had a gardener and occasionally my mother used her parents' chauffeur until she was able to purchase her own car. My dad had a company car which was replaced every two years. I was not streetwise and not used to the 'rough and tumble'.

Shelley mentioned my plight to the Pastor who had previously visited me at the hostel. He apparently took into consideration that I had always tithed despite my circumstances, not that this was the reason I tithed, and suggested that I look for privately rented accommodation.

It was a very cold December and we had already spent six months in the hostel. Shelley took me around in her car several times to help me find a house for rent. Weeks later and after seeing five properties, we eventually viewed a property which, on entering the hallway, I sensed that this was where we should reside. The tenancy agreement was for three years. It was clean, tidy and nicely decorated. Apparently the landlord spent a week cleaning it out after the previous tenants. I knew that he would not have a problem with me. The three bedroom semi-detached house was situated within a few minutes walk of the shops, public transport, an evangelical church and the school Josh was attending. Vikki was on the waiting list to join in a few months. It was ideal and a real blessing. The security deposit, equivalent to a month's rent was paid for me by my Pastor as a gift from the Church and the Estate agent who showed us the house, said that he would wait for the Housing Benefit Office to pay the monthly rent. As a result, we were able to move into the house without having to borrow any money for the deposit and security. God said He would provide and He was faithful to His Word.

20. PURSUING A DIVORCE

On the seventh day of January 1994, we moved into the three-bedroom semi detached house having spent seven months in the hostel. I had come to know that Biblically, the number seven is the number of perfection. God is so good and I really believe that He was reassuring me that even though I was going through hard and trying times, He was always right there beside me. In all, I had no control over the day we left the house which was the seventh day of June; the length of time we were in the hostel which was seven months nor the day we left the hostel which was the seventh of January; 777!! Isn't God just amazing?

The day was cold and the snowfall was heavy and slushy. The leader of the fellowship group and Shelley helped us in transporting all our belongings to our new abode. All our other possessions that were kept in storage for the past seven months were also delivered to the new address. The house was partially furnished with curtains in each bedroom, sitting room and dining room, fitted wardrobes in each bedroom and a fitted kitchen which housed a washing machine, tumble dryer, fridge, cooker and a freezer larder. There was a comfortably large rear garden and a smaller front garden with a driveway.

Being as organised as I am, it only took a matter of hours before all the rooms except the dining room, were sorted and ready for use. All the unopened boxes were neatly placed in the dining room. Karl brought us a most welcome take away which saved me thinking of what to cook for us and while we tucked into the tasty chicken and chips, I told him that he would have free access to the children but that he might prefer to join us for the evening meal when the children would have arrived home from school. It was about ten thirty that evening when he left and the children and I retired to bed but not before our prayer time. I was shattered and ached all over but there was so much for which I had to thank God. By the end of the first week, I had unpacked the boxes that were in the dining room and placed the contents in their appropriate places. Everywhere was clean and tidy and mentally, I felt relaxed.

One morning when the children left for school, I began to reflect on what my Pastor told me about divorcing Karl and also on the conflicting information my fellowship group leader gave me. I was confused and decided to fast and pray for clarity and wisdom in making the right decision. It was just after midday when the doorbell rang. A man who said he was a representative from the electric company who supplied the electricity to our marital home, was looking for Karl. When I told him that we were separated and living apart from each other, he said that there was an outstanding bill for which he would hold me accountable, if he were unable to locate Karl at the address I had given him. I told him that I was a Christian and would pay any outstanding debts concerning me but that at this time I was unemployed, living in rented accommodation, had no savings and was on Income Support.

By the time the representative was about to leave, I felt convinced in my spirit that the Lord was saying to me that I should pursue the divorce. At no time prior to getting married had I ever encountered any financial problems and now that I had the opportunity of rebuilding my life, it only seemed apt that I should manage my affairs and no longer allow Karl to do so. Often I heard my father say, "So you make your bed, so you would lie on it"; or "Do not beg, borrow or steal"; or "If you can't afford it, do without it". He did not encourage me with Christian values but he taught me to always make do with whatever I had.

When the representative left, I took the ten-minute walk into the high street hoping to find a firm of solicitors. The estate agent who was in charge of collecting the rent from me while the landlord and his family lived abroad, said that there were no solicitors' firms in the area but that they could give me the details of the nearest one. I followed this up but they did not deal with clients who required legal aid. They in turn gave me the details of another firm many miles away near to the Bed and Breakfast accommodation from which we had just moved. I rang the firm and an appointment was made for me to see a solicitor who I eventually found out was a Christian. Again I felt a strong confirmation that it was not wrong to pursue the divorce. During my first consultation, he stated that the case appeared to be straight-forward, that I should not have to go to the Courts and that it should take about six to eight weeks.

21. THE JOY OF FAMILY WORSHIP

Karl visited the children everyday, Monday to Friday and ate with us. We always sat at the table and said the "Grace" before eating. It was after one of these meals and before he left that I told him that I had filed for a divorce. I felt very tense assuming that he would display his anger as he had done in the past when I had threatened to leave him but he said and did nothing. I continued to correspond with my solicitor and kept all the necessary appointments. The children saw their dad at least six days in the week. He continued to join us for our main meal and take us to Church then on to my mother's for Sunday lunch. I also kept him updated with the children's education and took him with me to the Parent Teachers' Evenings when we would be informed of their educational progress.

One day Josh was sent home earlier from school owing to an injury to his shoulder which he sustained during PE. I gave him a pain-killing tablet for the pain and allowed him to rest until I had finished the cooking. Karl arrived and went up to Josh's bedroom to check on him while Vikki and I stayed in the kitchen preparing the meal. When we were ready to eat, I stood at the bottom of the stairs and called out to Karl and Josh telling them that we were ready to eat. When I had no response, I went up to the bedroom only to find that they were asleep. It was a most beautiful sight to behold. Josh was lying on his left side with Karl lying alongside facing Josh's back and with his arm around Josh's waist. I smiled and walked away quietly hoping not to disturb them. Vikki and I sat down to eat and later Karl and Josh had theirs.

Six weeks went by but my solicitor had had no response from the three sets of papers he had posted to Karl and I never brought up the subject when he visited. As a result, he had to be served the papers by a bailiff. However, he continued his visits and took us to Church every Sunday and I continued to tithe from my Income

Support. In making sure that all my 'paper work' was in order, one day I decided to list all of my expenses which excluded food and gasped as I noted that my outgoings exceeded my income. Although my husband gave the children pocket money, he had lost his business and was in no way able to support us financially. I reflected on what the Lord told us in April 1993, "...don't be afraid, I will provide for you and your children."

The months drifted by and as the summer approached, it was so beautiful to have a garden in which to sit out, relax and enjoy the beauty and colour of the plants and flowers. Vikki, who was now eleven, was looking forward to joining Josh at his school in September and had her uniform all prepared since the beginning of June. Josh was fifteen and I bought him a mobile phone with a tariff which allowed him to make free calls after seven o'clock in the evening and all day at the week ends to land lines. I also gave him a set of keys to the front door and allowed him to go out but to return at a reasonable time. Karl did not agree to this. However, my father had not allowed me to go out other than to school, church and ballet. I could not have a boyfriend or wear make-up. I was not allowed to receive telephone calls unless my father 'interrogated' the caller. If the caller was male and I was allowed to speak to him, my father would stand beside me as I talked making me feel most uncomfortable. I wanted my children to know that I loved them and trusted them to be responsible and law-abiding. I did not want them to have an upbringing like mine.

Every evening before bedtime we continued to have family worship but on one occasion Vikki and I decided to start without Josh because he was out with his friends. Just as we sat on my bed and were about to begin singing, the phone rang. It was Josh. "Have you started prayers?" he asked. When I told him we were just about to begin, he said that he was about five minutes' walk away and that we should wait for him. No sooner had he arrived, he got hold of his guitar and we began singing praises to Jesus.

God is so good. It was always a joy to see the delight on the children's faces as we prepared for worship.

22. OVERWHELMED WITH JOY

In September 1994, Vikki was eleven and now eligible to join Josh at his school. Each month brought its 'ups and downs' but through the trials God, I believe, was teaching me to trust Him. My mother suggested that I should try and find a job. The trauma I had been through still had me feeling very weak mentally and physically and I wondered if I was ready to face the world once again. I had now been out of work for sixteen months and felt I had lost all self-confidence in my ability to return to work.

However, I prayed and said, "Lord, if You want me to go back to work, You must 'spell' it out in bold black and white letters". Just a week had gone by when I was reading the free local paper which was put through my letterbox. I could not believe what I was seeing before me. It was an advert written in bold black and white letters for a part-time Matron (school nurse) at a local college. I have the cutting to this day. I was awe struck; God is truly amazing. This would be perfect because I would be with the children whenever they were at home – evenings, weekends and holidays. I could continue to go to Church every Sunday, something I could not do when I worked at the hospital. The job itself would be much less challenging than that of a ward sister's post and being part time, it would obviously be less stressful.

When I was five, we were being taught to write letters at school. My letter was to my mother telling her that I wanted to be a nurse to look after children and babies when I grew up. At the age of nine, when I mentioned this to a family friend, he told me that if I want to be a nurse, I should not stop until I attained the title of Matron. However, the nursing administrative levels changed five years into my training and the title of Matron was no longer in existence in General hospitals. Psalm 139 states, "…All the days ordained for me were written in Your book before one of them came to be". God is truly "the

Alpha and the Omega, the First and the Last, the Beginning and the End" Revelation chapter 22 verse 12. He knew exactly what He had planned for me. "For I know the plans I have for you" Jeremiah chapter 29 verse 11.

I felt a surge of excitement and rang for an application form. It was only a few days after I returned the form, that I had a telephone call from the Headmistress' secretary informing me that I had been short-listed and asking me to attend an interview in January before the start of the school term.

Autumn was drawing in fast and the local supermarket was inundated with just about everything to do with Christmas. Once all the monthly bills were paid by direct debit or standing order, there was very little left for groceries. Normally, I would only purchase what was on my shopping list but the children often asked for their favourite sweets, etc.. At the checkout, I would divide the groceries into two or three sections; the first section had the items we really needed; the second, was what we hoped we could afford and the third was usually something of the children's favourites. We always managed to get through the first section and very rarely did we get beyond the second section. However, this time the children asked for Christmas crackers and other Christmas stuff. When I told them that we would have to leave Christmas for the following year, they gracefully accepted. They were really amazing because they never once complained.

Although the neighbours on both sides of our home kept themselves to themselves, I decided to give them each a Christmas card which we put through their letterbox. Three days later we received a card from the family on the left of us. Then one evening, two weeks before Christmas, while we were having family worship, someone put something through our letterbox. I told Vikki that it must be a card from the other neighbour. She hurriedly jumped off the bed, scurried down the stairs and brought up an envelope addressed to me.

I was puzzled as I opened the envelope. In it was a note that stated, "Dear Pat, the Lord wants you to have this money. Matthew chapter 6 verse 25 – 34". Together with the note, which I have to this day, there were five twenty-pound notes. The children and I were speechless. The note was signed "anonymous". Wide-eyed I stared at the notes in my hand and wondered who could have done this. I was still having difficulty receiving and remember asking God to show me who did this generous act so that I could at least say thanks; but I realized later that this is not how God operates. He said He would provide for us and this is what He was doing. We carried on with our prayers, thanked God for His amazing provision and asked His blessings on the person who had given us the money. The following day I took the children to do some Christmas shopping and all they had asked for initially, they were now able to buy. What was even more amazing, was that there was enough left over for them to buy presents for their father, me and to exchange presents between themselves. I bought them each a present and for myself, a pair of earrings which cost twenty pounds, something I could ill afford without the generous gift we received.

A few days later, a man whom I had only recently met, paid me an impromptu visit. He said that someone had donated a six-foot artificial Christmas tree complete with all the decorations to his shop and he asked me if I would like to have it. "Yes, please," I said excitedly. "God is just amazing", I thought. There was no way financially, that we could have afforded all the trimmings of Christmas but God made a promise to us that He would provide and in His faithfulness, He provided much more than we could ever have asked for or imagined we would have had. Ephesians chapter 3 verses 20 and 21 state, "Now to Him who is able to do immeasurably more than all we ask or imagine, according to His power that is at work within us, to Him be glory in the church and in Christ Jesus throughout all generations, for ever and ever! Amen."

We, that is, my mother, the two children and myself

joined my brother and his family in Colchester for lunch on Christmas Day as we had done for the previous two years. My sister-in-law is excellent at preparing tasty, mouth-watering meals and this just rounded off a wonderful Christmas time. I give all honour, praise and glory to my Lord and Saviour, Jesus Christ.

23. BEREAVED

January 1995 I attended the interview which seemed to go well although I felt a twinge of doubt. Immediately after the interview, I popped into the local supermarket to get a few items. I was still having problems with my back and always used a small trolley even for a few items instead of a basket. I fetched a trolley and it was more convenient to put my handbag strap over my head, on my shoulder and across my chest. As I passed the strap over my head, it caught my 'expensive' earring on my left ear and it fell to the ground. Immediately, I found the earring and I looked everywhere within a reasonable radius of where I located the earring but could not find the butterfly which holds the earring in place.

After five minutes or more I gave up looking for it. It was the best pair of earrings I had and they were barely a month old. "How could this happen?" I thought. As I pushed my trolley into the supermarket, I felt the Lord say to me that I should not worry but trust Him in all things. I remember saying to myself, "It's only an earring. God is good. He'll provide another one for me". I spent about half an hour in the supermarket and by the time I was about to leave, it was beginning to turn dark. The lights in the forecourt were on and I had thought no more about the earring because I gave up on ever finding it. Anyway, the butterfly was so small, it would have easily been trampled on and be of no further use.

As I entered the forecourt, ahead of me on the ground, there was a sparkle. I walked towards it and as I stooped down to look at it, it was the butterfly!! Dozens of people would have entered and left the supermarket. Surely they would have trampled on it. But the butterfly was intact as if untouched. I was amazed. Trusting God at all times and in all things is not always easy but He does have a gentle, loving way of helping us to learn to trust Him. I smiled as

I felt His tangible presence walking alongside me. "Thank you Jesus", I said and made my way home.

The day following the interview, I had a telephone call informing me that I was the successful applicant of the three of us who applied for the post. In January 1995, I started my new job as the Head Matron of the college and met Jo and Nancy, the other two Matrons. Jo worked part time, filling the two days that I was not working and Nancy covered us for our lunch breaks. We worked very well together and eventually became good friends. Their support and genuine friendship quickly helped me to regain my self-confidence and I settled quickly into a routine that was very different to that of working in a hospital.

Although the annual wage was approximately eight thousand pounds less than my previous post, everything about this job was perfect for my needs at the time. God said that He would provide and I was seeing His amazing faithfulness in doing so. My divorce came through one month after I started working at the college. Karl continued his relationship with the children as before. Nothing really changed. My mother who displayed a sense of relief now that I could possibly be starting a new chapter in my life, died six months later. We had become friends in the previous two years before her death. I was shocked and devastated. This was my first experience of the death of someone so close to me. However, I had the peaceful reassurance that because she gave her life to Jesus two years earlier, she was now in Heaven and when I die I will see her again.

My mother had had a coronary by-pass operation fifteen years prior to her death. She had come over to the UK for private treatment and during the time she was in hospital, my father divorced her. He rang her several times during her stay in the hospital and sent her flowers; so, after her recovery when she returned to the West Indies, she told me that she was shocked to find a letter on her dressing table informing her that my father had divorced her without giving her any opportunity to contest.

My mother had been on the waiting list for a second coronary by-pass and when she was given a date in August 1995 to go into hospital, she asked me to accompany her. My mother was seventy-one years of age, very attractive and looked much younger than her age. Vikki and I went over to her flat where I helped her to pack a small suitcase before we set off for Hammersmith Hospital where we stayed with her until visiting was over. My intention was to visit her the following day after the operation but she died during surgery.

24. HARROWING SITUATIONS

The children were now twelve and sixteen years of age respectively and we decided to leave our church which was about eight miles away and join the local evangelical church which was within easy walking distance from where we lived. The warmth and love we felt at this church helped us to settle in quickly to a family of new friends; friends like Richard and Kate who supported us and prayed for us during the very difficult times. I also became an ardent listener of a recently launched Christian radio station whether I was at home, at work or in the car. A friend of my mother's had given her a car of which I was a named driver. When she died I inherited it. This was a real blessing especially when doing the weekly groceries because I was finding the strain on my back becoming more intolerable.

Despite the stresses of day to day living, working, managing my finances on a very low budget and bringing up the two children on my own, we continued to have family worship before bedtime and attend church every Sunday. I also continued to attend the fellowship group from my previous church and contributed by fetching three of the elderly women, taking them to the meetings and then back to their respective homes. I also spent some of my time during my days off from work visiting one of these ladies who was disabled and lived alone in a first floor flat. It was during one of these visits that she requested my help in getting her in and out of the bathtub for a weekly bath, something she looked forward to because, as she told me, the carer only gave her a wash.

All my friend could see from her chair in her sitting room was the sky. I remember her telling me that she could not tell whether it was raining or not and that the only time she saw her garden was when she went out which was not frequent. My heart went out to this dear woman and I felt a great desire to give her more of my time as it brought her so much happiness. We chatted about almost everything and laughed a lot. She did not hesitate to accept my offer to take her out. Sometimes we went for a drive, or to a church fete, or for a walk. At the outset, she used a walking frame but as her condition grew worse, she was forced to use a wheelchair. Although pushing the wheelchair and lifting it into and out of the boot of the car was taxing on my back, I saw her needs as greater than mine and continued to visit her until she passed away.

Being a committed Christian did not exempt me from the many harrowing situations I frequently faced in addition to the daily stresses. Situations such as Josh having suspected meningitis; being caught up in a house fire while visiting his friend and having to seek the assistance of a solicitor to deal with the case; Vikki whose hand blew up like a balloon when she fell down the staircase and having to be rushed to hospital. Another occasion occurred when Josh had not yet arrived home from going out with his friends and Vikki and I had already settled for bed. I was asleep when the telephone rang. It was Josh. He had given his bus ticket to one of the girls in the group and began walking home. He asked me to come and meet him when he was about two blocks away. I did not like being out in the dark and felt a great deal of apprehension when the children were out after dark. My heart was pounding fast as I hurriedly put on a coat over my nightdress and rushed out to the car that was covered with snow. In my anxiety to get to Josh as quickly as possible, I did not waste time removing the snow from the car. A small area on the windscreen, which just about allowed me to see where I was going, was created with the fan set on high and the wipers in motion. Visibility was reduced as I peered through the semi circular clearance just above the dashboard and drove in the direction to meet him. It was such a relief to see him and to know that he was safe.

Two days later I woke up as usual for work. As I sat up

with my feet on the floor and before I could stand up, I felt as if a violent wind had struck me and I fell backwards on the bed. I lay on the bed wondering if I was dreaming. With my eyes closed, my arms and legs felt as if they were spinning like the blades of a helicopter. I opened my eyes only to find that my arms and legs were not moving. It was a frightening experience and I had no idea what was happening. I stood up and although feeling extremely dizzy, I continued to get ready for work being careful not to turn my head to the left or right as this movement worsened the dizziness. I felt weak as I prayed and asked God to sustain and protect me. I should have had the day off from work but a sense of guilt overcame me; guilt of not being able to maintain standards that were expected of me. A subsequent visit to my GP revealed a diagnosis of labyrinthitis probably as a result of stress.

With all of the above in a short space of time, I also sustained an accident at work. I was walking back to the sick bay from the swimming pool area when I walked into the double glazed, ceiling to floor glass door leading to the exit causing the whole pane to be shattered. No immediate pain was apparent and I was able to walk back to the office and report that I had had an accident. As I sat down I became aware of the excruciating pain which radiated down both arms with any movement or the slightest touch anywhere along my arms. An emergency telephone call brought an ambulance to the school. A neck brace was fitted and I was taken to the ambulance on a trolley. Every jolt caused me extreme pain. I was taken to the local hospital where a diagnosis of severe whiplash was made and remained an inpatient for ten days.

My cousin, who had come to the UK from the West Indies to attend my mother's funeral and was staying at my home, looked after the children. Every day Karl brought them to visit me at the hospital. The whiplash was so severe that I was unable to touch anything without experiencing pain. Simple tasks such as holding my toothbrush or comb or a doorknob produced pain. As a result whenever the children and their father visited, I took the opportunity to have them help me with having a shower. The children seemed to see the funny side of seeing their dad smear me with soap bubbles while they jetted the spray of water all over me.

Isaiah chapter 43 verse 2 states, "When you pass through the waters, I will be with you; and when you pass through the rivers, they will not sweep over you. When you walk through the fire, you will not be burned; the flames will not set you ablaze." Through all the upheavals, the pain and the suffering I knew that the Lord was with us because I always felt an inner joy and peace. A peace and joy that allowed me to put aside my problems and care for those who were in need, or to entertain an impromptu visit by a friend with whom I could share a meal or just be a listening ear.

One day the children and I had just said the 'Grace' prior to eating our evening meal when the doorbell rang. A friend from my previous church paid us an impromptu visit. He had not had his evening meal and I had not started on mine. I offered my portion to him and left him to eat with the children while I began to prepare something else for myself. This sharing of food was something I enjoyed and the more I did, the more blessed I felt. I remember my grandmother saying that she never threw away left over food until the following day just in case someone who was hungry came by late in the evening and she could offer him or her something to eat. I recall another occasion when we were already settled in bed for the night and doorbell rang. It was another friend from my previous church. He was on his way home from work and had not eaten. I got the pots and pans out and began cooking a meal for him. After dessert and a cup of tea, he left. I smiled and praised God as I went up the stairs and back to bed. God is so good. I had so little, yet always had so much to give. Truly my cup was overflowing, (Psalm 23 Verse 5).

25. ANSWERED PRAYER

The tenancy agreement on the house was three years, which seemed a long time when we moved in but the months went by very quickly and we had now been living there for two years and ten months. The estate agent served me a two-month notice to leave according to the agreement. I had had a good rapport with the landlord who inspected the property whenever he was in the UK. He told me that he had had no complaints from the neighbours about us or from the estate agent who collected the monthly rent on his behalf. He also told me that I had maintained the house in a clean and tidy manner.

Very soon after I was given the notice, the 'For Sale' board was put in situ in front of the house. Being a single woman and having a young teenage daughter, I felt a certain amount of apprehension about having lots of strangers in and out of the house. I prayed that God would only send the people who were genuinely interested in purchasing the property. A few hours after the advertising board was put in place, the estate agent rang to inform me that a Mr. X requested a viewing. When I was told that he was not a family man, I became a bit suspicious and refused to allow the viewing. The second request was that of a family who seemed to like the house but made no offer to purchase.

Shortly after the first viewing another family came to see the property. As the couple entered the house, the woman recognized Vikki from having met her three years prior. Before we lost our home, Vikki visited a school friend whose mum and dad took them, that is, Vikki and her friend, to visit another family. It was this family that were viewing the house. The woman told me that her son and his girl friend would be joining them any minute. Then the doorbell rang. As the son entered the hallway, the woman began to introduce her son to me. Immediately he stopped her and told her that he had been to the house many times before because he and Josh were friends. I do not believe that this was a coincidence. I truly believe that God is gracious and compassionate (Psalm 145 Verse 8) and He allayed my fears by sending a family with whom we or rather, Vikki had had some contact previously.

As they left the house and walked towards their car, I thanked God for His faithfulness in keeping His promise to us. He said "…. don't be afraid, I will provide for you and your children." God is so good. In a very short space of time, He provided a lovely family who had a subsequent viewing and made an offer to purchase the property thereby reducing the number of people who may have been interested in buying the house.

The landlord who had recently returned to the UK had given me lots of boxes which was thoughtful of him and a real blessing. The children and I began to pack all our belongings leaving unpacked, the very bare necessities. I began looking for somewhere to live; somewhere within easy reach of where I worked, the children's school and the church. I felt confident because God said He would provide and the church continued to pray for us on a regular basis. I also got a lot of comfort from listening to the Christian radio station. What I found really amazing was, on quite a number of occasions God spoke directly into my circumstances through some of the sermons I listened to on the radio. I therefore decided to keep the radio on even while I slept and incredible though it may sound, I often dreamt that I was singing a worship song or I would be listening to someone who was telling me about the Lord.

Every day I checked the local paper and friends at the church helped by telling me of properties they knew of or owned. When I found a suitable property, I informed the Housing Benefit office. I was already in receipt of Housing Benefit owing to my low income and thought that it would have been straightforward to continue with the facility when I moved into another property but it turned out to be a nightmare. I was back and forth from the office and almost pleading with the officers to understand my desperate situation. I was beginning to feel greatly stressed as the weeks were going by and I had not found anywhere to live. Christmas was a few weeks away, not that I was able to entertain the thought of celebrating the event. The estate agent rang frequently to check on my progress and was not pleased when I was unable to give them positive news. I took the threat of having all my belongings put out onto the road if I did not leave, very seriously. The children and I continued to pray but with nothing in sight, I was beginning to wilt. In vain I tried not to worry but I was feeling the consequence of the amount of stress I suffered.

My sleep pattern grew worse and I was sleeping for approximately two to three hours every night. Most nights I would lie awake gazing at the ceiling and wondering where was God in all of this as the warm trickle of tears effortlessly flowed. One sleepless night, I decided to read my Bible. With no particular chapter in mind, I randomly opened the Bible and noted a passage which stood out like a bright light. It was Revelation chapter 2 verses 9 and 10 which state, "I know your afflictions and your poverty – yet you are rich! ...... Do not be afraid of what you are about to suffer." I did not search for these verses, they simply stood out as if they were the only words on the page. This was amazing. A smile filled my countenance and I blurted out, "God really, really knows all about me." It is so easy to pray and read God's Word and tell yourself that you believe in Him but when you are faced with difficult times and He tells you that He knows exactly what is happening, it can be so reassuring and exciting. Psalm 139 verse 16 states, "Your eyes saw my unformed body. All the days ordained for me were written in your book before one of them came to be." God who knows all about me was reassuring me that He was with me in all my afflictions and suffering.

As stated at the outset, I had read the Bible from cover to

cover before introducing the children to having it read to them. When we began having family worship, we read a chapter or part every night. However, if Josh could not be in at the time Vikki and I were ready to say our prayers, we would read a psalm or a random verse so as not to have Josh miss the continuity that he had established. One evening when the three of us were having our fellowship, I read 2 Samuel, chapter 7. When I got to verse ten it stated, "And I will provide a place for my people Israel and will plant them so that they can have a home of their own and no longer be disturbed." Immediately I felt the Lord say to me that we should not worry and that He would provide a permanent home for us. This was so exciting. I immediately underlined the verse putting the date next to it and re-read it to the children replacing Israel with our names. What I also found remarkable was that this date was the last day of the two-month notice we were given to leave the house. With all our belongings packed for the past two months and the hope of finding a place remote, God 'steps' in and basically tells us He is in control, don't worry, He WILL provide.

On the following Sunday at church, I was asked by one of the parishioners if we had found somewhere to move to; excitably, my confident answer was, "No, not yet but the Lord told us that He WILL provide a place for us so that we could have a home of our own and no longer be disturbed." God does not make mistakes; He is simply amazing.

26. ANOTHER MOVE

Eventually we were offered temporary housing in a second floor flat in a three storey building seven miles away from the children's school and from where I worked in an area unfamiliar to us but not before I was taken to court. I found this experience to be a most terrifying and embarrassing ordeal which caused me to be greatly stressed. However, together with the pastor and an elder of the church and two of the service support team from the school where I worked, we transported all our belongings to our new home.

The building had one communal entry and had been a home for girls on remand. It was recently refurbished and being used for homeless families. The newly magnolia painted walls, new carpets throughout the building and new fittings made the very spacious flat look clean and tidy as we put all the furniture in their appropriate positions immediately on off loading the vans. Again and as before, every room was complete apart from Vikki's bedroom where we stored all the boxes to be unpacked. It took five days to have the contents of all the boxes put in their appropriate places and every room organized.

The kitchen was fitted with newly built cupboards and a kitchen sink. It was not furnished with necessities such as a cooker, fridge, freezer or washing machine and until I was able to afford these items, I made the arduous journey with two large bags of washing to the laundry once a week. Being more familiar with the area from which we had just moved it was easier for me to drop the children off to school on my day off from work and then do the laundry. Every day I had to buy milk and other foods which would normally be kept in a fridge or freezer and manage on microwave foods until soon after moving in, we acquired a second hand cooker. It is so easy to take certain comforts for granted until one is deprived of them. Having the cooker seemed a luxury and it was almost a year before I was able to afford a washing machine and a fridge/freezer.

I was grateful for somewhere to live; however, there were many problems which affected me adversely. I was concerned that there was no fire escape route other than the front door of the flat. The large, sealed picture windows had very small openings above them which would not have allowed us a route of escape in the event of a fire occurring in the flat adjacent to our front door. I was also fearful for myself and the children of the intimidation posed by the groups of youths who idled around the stair well especially during the evenings. There were times when I had to call the police because of the fights that broke out among them and it was not long before the walls were covered in graffiti and empty beer cans and other litter strewn around the staircase.

The flat adjacent to my front door was unoccupied until a single young man moved in. He eventually sublet the flat to two females who were involved in what seemed to be an illegal business. During the late evening, at night and sometimes during the day, there was a queue of men who were constantly in and out of the flat. The disturbance during the night was unbelievable. The banging of the door every half an hour as it closed behind the 'clients', gave an indication of the time they arrived and left.

I often found myself heavy with worry if the children, especially Vikki, were due to arrive home on their own especially after dark. One afternoon, I was walking back to the flat having just got off the bus and walked passed a youth who was sitting on a bench near the bus stop. He muttered something as I went by. I did not respond but his response was to get up and follow me. As he closed in, I felt uncomfortable and began to run heading for the main door of the building. Fortunately, the door which should have been locked had been left open. I ran into the building and shut the door leaving him on the outside. I was breathless and trembling with fear of what could have happened to me or if it were Vikki.

I was still in receipt of housing benefit but was overwhelmed by the problems I encountered in dealing with the office. I kept meticulous files of all my documents; I was honest in all the information I disclosed to them; I always informed them immediately of any changes in my circumstances and promptly handed in documents they requested instead of posting them. However, on the occasions when I had letters informing me that I had been overpaid or of an accusation of some error on my part, caused me added stress. The hours spent in taking my files to the office and waiting to be seen only to have confirmation that I was not in error and had not defaulted, seemed so unnecessary. I recall having received a summons from the court. I was waiting at the main door for a friend with whom I took turns in driving to church, when I glanced at the tenants' mail in a bundle on the floor. Prior to this, we had our mail delivered to each flat. Curiosity made me look through the bundle for my mail. I was shocked to open a letter stating that there was a summons for me to attend court for the non-payment of money owed to the housing benefit office. It was a matter that I had dealt with previously and they admitted that they were at fault and no further action was to be taken.

My friend arrived. Mentally and physically I felt very weak. I tried not to worry but the stress weighed heavily on me. On the way to church, I mentally drafted a letter to the magistrate in response to the summons. I wrote the letter on my return from church itemising the number of times the benefit office had made mistakes concerning my affairs. I stated that I was already under a tremendous amount of stress and that their errors only added to the burden. I went on to say that the office should be summoned to court. I guess I was angry as I penned those words. I heard no further from the benefit office nor did I have a reply from the magistrate.

Knowing Jesus as your Lord and Saviour is not a ticket to a trouble free life. John chapter 16 verse 33 states, "….

In this world you will have trouble. But take heart! I have overcome the world."

27. TOTAL DESPAIR

I would hardly have got over one stressful episode when I was faced with another. In addition to insomnia, backache and sciatica, I began to suffer with gastric problems and persistent headache. It was about this time that I had my first MRI scan on my back. The report stated that I had severe degenerative bone disease of my lower back. I was also diagnosed with trigger finger of my thumb and middle finger on my right hand. One evening I had a massive nose bleed which lasted six hours and was rushed by ambulance to the local hospital. A diagnosis of high blood pressure was made and subsequently my GP commenced me on anti-hypertensive therapy. My sleep pattern, which varied between one and three hours every night was diagnosed as severe insomnia for which my GP prescribed sleeping tablets. During the many hours, sometimes up to five, of turning and tossing, I tried in vain to focus on the programmes on the Christian radio station in order to be distracted from the turmoil that invaded my thoughts. Reading or getting out of bed and tackling a household chore did not work either. Owing to the lack of adequate sleep, I was always tired and felt as if I had done a day's work by nine o'clock in the morning. Therefore, whenever I was on my day off I often took the opportunity to have a lie-in.

One such morning when I turned over and pulled the duvet up over my shoulders and snuggled in between the sheets, Vikki who was awake and getting herself ready for school, came into my bedroom. She said that she could not remove a ring from her finger. She had put the ring on the day before and slept with it. Her first attempt to take it off failed. As a result, she desperately pulled at it causing her finger to swell. "Well," I said with a deep sigh, "I guess I would have to take you to the hospital to have it cut off." I could not understand why she almost became hysterical until I realized that she thought that she would have to have her finger cut off. That morning I obviously did not get my longed for lie-in.

Karl's visits were infrequent and I virtually had no support from him; instead, I was faced with financial problems that he should have dealt with but he palmed them on to me. It cost me umpteen telephone calls to and visits to my home from the creditors before the matter was passed back to him. I was mother and father to the children and on no occasion did he ever have them for a day, a weekend or a holiday. Josh was in his late teens and our relationship was being greatly stretched. I sought help from my pastor who said that it was just a phase that all teenage boys go through. I felt so despondent. I did not have the resources to take him and Vikki on a holiday or buy him the clothes and shoes he needed. Often he wore clothes borrowed from his friends. I felt I had failed my children. This constant worry of how to compensate for all they missed out on really stressed me. I was drained; I felt that I could no longer cope; I really wanted to die. Then, the thought of the children and their future without their mother, flashed through my mind. "O God, please forgive me; how could I be so selfish," I thought and begged God to sustain me.

Vikki was preparing for her GCSE's. Unlike Josh who had a very high IQ, Vikki was of average intelligence and worked hard but needed support. I was burdened with a tremendous amount of stress but knew that I had to help her. I recall one evening when she was doing her course work in English Literature and I had to read one of the novels on the suggested list in order to help her with the questions. I read the first page of the novel and realized that I could not make sense of what I had read because of the mental block due to stress. However, I persisted, sometimes working with her to early hours in the morning. The persistence paid off and she subsequently attained the grades she required for entry to the London College of Fashion where she eventually graduated with a Batchelor of Arts (Honours) degree in men's wear fashion design.

The children were now in their late teens and family worship was not as regular as before because they were either out late or on a sleep over when I was ready for my prayer time. Occasionally Vikki and I would pray together but more often that not, I prayed on my own. Despite my regular attendance at church and at a fellowship group I recently joined, the heavy stress load made me feel as if the Lord was distant from me. The group were very supportive in praying for me through the difficult times and I was beginning to feel the Lord's presence once again until a broken relationship almost led me to a mental breakdown.

Yet it was during these darkest times that I led people to the Lord and gave away Bibles, but struggled when the Lord told me to tithe from my gross income. I kept a regular check on my outgoings against my income and it was on one of these occasions when the Lord told me in my spirit to stop tithing from my net income and start tithing from my gross. "How can I, Lord? We can hardly manage on what we have." Then as in a flash, I recalled, "...don't be afraid, I will provide for you and your children." Immediately, I felt a sense of surrender. "Lord," I said, "I will. You have been so good to me, how can I not trust You."

Just when I thought that I was beginning to cope, the twenty-five year old automatic Saab car that we had been using decided it had done its time. A friend who worked at the school with me and lived close by, offered to give the children and me a lift every morning, dropping the children off at a bus stop near the school thereby allowing them to take one bus instead of the three buses that they would normally take. One evening in our prayer time we prayed for a car. A few days after that prayer, I was out shopping when I bumped into a friend whom I had not seen for a long time. During our chat, I mentioned that I no longer had a car. He told me that a couple who had recently purchased a brand new Yugo, had gone to Uganda for a year as missionaries and had offered their car to anyone in the church who needed it. No one took up this offer and for many months, the car was parked up at the Pastor's home. "Was God keeping the car for us?" I wondered. Following a telephone call to the Pastor, I went over to his home where I was handed the keys of the car that we would have for one year.

It was October and we had been using the Yugo for ten months. I was conscious of the fact that we would be handing back the car to the owners who were due to return to the UK in two months time. Vikki and I prayed for a car. A week later, the sister of my Pastor rang. It was a Saturday morning and I was in bed reading my Bible. Initially I did not recognise her voice because we were not regularly in touch. However, after enquiring about the children, she asked me if I would like to have a car. For a moment I thought I was dreaming and sat bolt upright in the bed to make sure of what I had heard. She said that a friend of hers had recently died and she inherited the friend's four-door car which was more suitable for her two children as they were now older. She no longer had any use for the two door white Ford estate and wished to give it away. Excitedly I accepted. Mark chapter 11 verse 24 states, "Therefore I tell you, whatever you ask for in prayer, believe that you have received it, and it will be yours."

28. GOD'S FAITHFULNESS

It was now a total of seven years that we were living in temporary housing and three years and ten months at this present home when I received a letter from a Housing Association inviting me to attend an interview. By now I was so stressed, I barely had the physical or mental energy to go on but for the grace and strength of the Lord. I had lost a lot of weight; I was using prescribed sleeping tablets to help me sleep and the pain in my lower back and down my leg was unbearable. However, on the morning of the interview, I asked Vikki to pray with me. My prayer was short and simple, "Dear Lord, please give us a nice home with nice neighbours, in Jesus Name." And we both said "Amen," which means, "So be it."

It was raining heavily when Richard and Kate, who offered to take me to the interview, arrived to fetch me. After Narinder, the housing manager took some details and filled in all the necessary papers she said that the association were in the process of building new property near to where I worked and that she would like to offer me a three double bedroom house which should be ready in approximately four months. Kate, who accompanied me to the interview room and I, heard what was said but I felt as if I were dreaming. "Could this be real," I thought. On the way back to the flat, the words, "We would like to offer you a three double bedroom house", kept going through my mind but even then it did not sink in until much later.

I was taken back to the flat and after having a hot drink and a short chat, Richard and Kate left. The children were at school and I was alone. I felt weak and worn out but had the desire to go to my bedroom and read my Bible which was near the radio on my bedside table. I took up the Bible from the table and simultaneously switched on the radio which remained programmed to the Christian radio station and heard, "God is faithful, God is faithful, God is faithful." The presenter who was speaking these words was described as having a golden voice. No one could imagine how amazing this was. I stood holding my Bible clutched to my chest in the stillness of my bedroom as I heard this 'golden' voice repeat three times, "God is faithful." There was no background music, just his voice repeating, "God is faithful." I promptly opened my Bible to the verse, "Don't be afraid, I will provide for you and your children." I gazed at the words as my eyes welled up with tears which cascaded down my face. I held the opened Bible to my chest and tried to thank God but I was speechless and in awe of His amazing grace. Ephesians chapter 3 verse 20 states, "Now to Him who is able to do immeasurably more than all we ask or imagine, according to His power that is at work within us, to Him be glory in the church and in Christ Jesus throughout all generations, for ever and ever! Amen." "Thank you, Jesus," I humbly said.

That night I had my prayer time alone because the children had been away for the weekend. Very coyly I prayed and asked the Lord for a large sum of money to purchase four items for the new house. These items were, a garden shed to store all my garden tools that a friend had been keeping for me; a shower unit because we preferred showers to baths; mixer taps in the kitchen and a downstairs toilet. I really had to trust God to provide because I had no savings, no credit facilities and was loathe to borrowing.

Subsequently, I was informed in writing of the property that I was offered at the interview. The months seemed to go by very quickly now that we could look forward to a permanent home. It was only a month before we were to move, when one morning on my day off I decided to have a 'lie-in'. I reached for my Bible on my bedside table. I opened it and immediately my eyes fell on a verse in the Book of Haggai. If I was ever reading the Bible on my own, I found a tremendous amount of comfort in the Psalms and this was my intention, to read the Psalms. But the Bible fell open in the Book of Haggai and verse 9 of chapter 2 stood out like a bright light. It was not even highlighted like some of the other verses. It stated, "The glory of this present house will be greater than the glory of the former house," says the Lord Almighty. "And in this place I will grant peace," declares the Lord Almighty.

My immediate reaction was, "Lord, why are You telling me that the glory of where we are presently residing, will be greater than the glory of the previous home?" Immediately I heard the silent voice of the Lord say, " I have already given you a home where you will no longer be disturbed, the new home that is being built for you. My glory and peace will go ahead of you." I had seen the hand of the Lord move in my life but this was, yes, truly amazing. I had no idea what the Lord had in store for me but the hope of another miracle was exciting.

29. MORE ANSWERED PRAYER

I received a letter from the housing association informing me of a date on which I should go over to the new property to pick up the keys and sign the necessary papers. I dropped Vikki off at school, which was a stone's throw from where the house was situated, and Josh accompanied me to the house. It was a beautiful, sunny day in December 2000 when we arrived at the property and were greeted by Narinder who was in the kitchen situated at the front of the house. She was preparing the forms for me to sign when she said, "Have a look around, it is your house." Gingerly, I walked out of the kitchen into the hallway with Josh on tow. There was a door on the left under the staircase which I assumed was a door to a larder. I opened the door and gasped, "It's a downstairs toilet."

I closed the door and walking ahead to the living room overlooking the rear garden, my eyes zoomed in to a garden shed that sat so beautifully in the top left hand corner of the garden. Already I had two of the four items for which I had asked the Lord. I remained composed although I wanted to spin around with arms wide open and shout, "Yippee!!!" The colour of the walls of the living / dining room was magnolia and the flooring was cream lino.

We proceeded to go upstairs. The staircase was bare wood and the flooring throughout the top floor was plasterboard. The colour scheme throughout the house was white and magnolia which are my favourite colours. Apart from builder's dust, every room looked clean, spacious and lovely. Just past the airing cupboard on the landing, Josh and I walked into the bathroom. There was a curtain rail in situ with a white waterproof curtain on the rail. I peered behind the curtain and my eyes almost popped out. I turned to Josh behind me and said with excitement, "There is a shower unit already plumbed in."

We proceeded to look at the three double bedrooms and

selected which one we each wanted, leaving no choice for Vikki; but everywhere was just so beautiful that it would not have mattered if we had to swap. The bedrooms Josh and I chose had built in wardrobes which were an added blessing. At the flat, we had a very large built in cupboard in Vikki's bedroom which we used as a wardrobe. Josh and I had free-standing single white wardrobes. This meant that Vikki's bedroom could have the two white wardrobes sitting side by side because her room was the only one without a built in wardrobe. I felt such a deep exciting thrill ripple through my body as we headed back down the stairs. I had asked my Lord and Saviour for the finance to purchase four specific items and so far He had provided three. I felt a broad smile fill my countenance as I whispered, "Thank you, Jesus."

We walked back to the very spacious kitchen where Narinder was standing with her back to the kitchen sink as she continued to pen through the paper work. I stood facing her and before signing the contract, I looked ahead of me and stared in unbelief at the mixer taps on the kitchen sink. All of the four items I had hoped to purchase with the money I had asked the Lord to provide were already in situ. On reflection, these items would have already been installed in the house even before I prayed for them. Matthew chapter 6 verse 8 states, "...for your Father knows what you need before you ask Him." I signed the forms in the respective places, was handed the keys and told, "This house is yours for life." This meant that if I died, the children would be allowed to continue to live at the house, provided of course, the rent was kept up to date.

I had access at the weekend to the property before the commencement of paying the rent. This gave me the opportunity to go back to the house on the following day with cleaning materials and thoroughly clean all the rooms, shelves and cupboards. After five hours of continuous cleaning, I was exhausted but thrilled that everywhere looked clean and tidy. With the generous help of Richard and Kate, we moved to our new permanent home and quickly settled in. God is so good.

30. A BRAND NEW CAR

Over the previous four years I had to take Vikki to Karl's home so that she could use his computer for her homework. Timidly, I approached Richard and Kate and told them that I would like to have a computer but that I could not afford to purchase one and asked if they were in a position to help me. They were delighted to assist and in monthly interest free instalments as they suggested, I paid them in return. A few weeks later, they purchased for me, a four-door Rover which was just three years old, to replace the Ford estate which was becoming expensive to maintain because of its age. I repaid them on the same basis as I did with the computer.

We had now been living at the house for five months when Josh applied to do a degree course in Music Performance. A few months before he temporarily moved to Brighton to begin his studies, I began a courtship which resulted in a marriage that lasted nineteen months. I not only lost my car, I was totally devastated by the trauma. For four months I was without the use of a car and suffered a great deal of backache and sciatica as I carried the heavy load of all my stuff for work and walked the twenty-minute journey from my home to the bus stop. It was a fifteen-minute journey on the bus, then a ten-minute walk to my place of work. I was grateful to the members of my fellowship group who helped by offering to take me to do my groceries. Once a week they would take it in turns to fetch Vikki and me, drive us to the supermarket and wait the hour or so for us to get through our shopping list. The strain on my back was intolerable. By the time Vikki and I arrived at the checkout, I could hardly stand upright because of the pain.

Then one day I had a telephone call from Kate informing me that one of the parishioners at her church was selling an 850cc Rover for five hundred pounds. I was the only 'bread winner' in the home and my income was much less than my outgoings. I was in arrears with my rent for which I was served a notice of repossession on two separate occasions. The thought of losing our home caused me a great deal of stress but I recalled the Lord telling me that He would give us a home where we would no longer be disturbed. I interpreted "disturbed" to mean that we would not move from or lose our home. The children were in full-time higher education and I had recently sent out applications for jobs. Eventually, I had the offer of two part-time jobs which I readily accepted. The income from doing three jobs and working seven days a week helped me pay off the arrears but I did not have the money to purchase the Rover. She reassured me that I should not worry and suggested that I telephone the owner of the car.

Before making the call, I thought I would pray about the matter; but before I finished praying, I had another call from Kate who said that the owner of the car no longer wanted to sell the car, he wanted to give it away. It became apparent that he was a car enthusiast and had just bought himself a Jaguar to replace the Rover. Up to this time neither he nor I thought that we knew each other. It was during the telephone call I made to him before going over to his home that we realized that we did know each other.

One Sunday, ten years prior to being given the car, the children and I had gone to church. I saw a young woman sitting on her own amidst the three hundred strong congregation. There was something that compelled me to go over to her and invite her to have Sunday lunch with us. I introduced myself to her and made the suggestion which she willingly accepted. At this time I had been a committed Christian for six years and the love of the Lord just flowed through me. I could only describe it as being on a 'high'. I shared this love with all whom I met from day to day with a bubbly excitement. However, soon after this visit, we lost our home and lost touch with each other. I was unaware that she had got married to someone who was a car enthusiast and who the Lord would use in giving me a car.

The car was described as the Rolls Royce of the Rovers. However, at twenty miles to the gallon, it was beautiful to drive but expensive to maintain. One day I took it to the garage to have a new exhaust fitted. While the fitting was being done, the mechanic noted that the rear tyres needed replacing. On my way back home I thanked God for the car but asked Him to provide the money to maintain it because it was becoming a strain on my income. About two months prior, I was in a lot of pain with my back and took some painkillers. I browsed through the local free magazine as I waited for some relief of the pain. I noted an article on the Blue Badge scheme which is of great benefit to the disabled. Although I did not think of myself as disabled, I felt that if I were entitled to one, it would be of help if only to avoid walking any distance while carrying a heavy load to or from my car.

Following the application for a Blue Badge, I had an independent assessment by an occupational therapist provided by the local council. During the interview and assessment, she suggested that I should apply for disability living allowance but I told her that I was not disabled. However, she gave me the telephone number and a subsequent call to the department led to the receipt of a bundle of forms which I duly completed and returned. This was followed by an examination by my GP. Before I had a response from the Department of Health and Social Security, I received the Blue Badge in the post and not long after that, information confirming my entitlement to disability living allowance was sent to me. This allowance was put towards a brand new car through Motability. I asked the Lord for the provision to maintain the Rover; instead, He gave me a brand new car. I shook my head in awe as I pondered on God's amazing grace which is so humbling.

31. BACK TO UNIVERSITY

In September 2005, I decided that after much prayer in seeking God's wisdom, I wanted to return to full-time nursing whereby I would work five days or the equivalent of thirty-seven and a half hours a week instead of trying to cope with three part-time jobs and working seven days a week. Owing to the chronic back problems that affected me, I thought it best to return to midwifery rather than paediatrics although I had not worked as a midwife for thirty-two years. Since graduating as a midwife in 1973, I had been working in nursing fields other than midwifery. So when I approached the university for an application form to attend the 'Return to Practice' course in midwifery, the tutor told me that she had not encountered anyone who had been out of the profession for as long as I and had taken on the challenge of returning. However, she accepted my application stating that the course would take six months unless I could not meet the deadlines, at which point she would allow me extended time.

I began the course in October 2005 attending university one day a week and working four days on the wards. One week into my course, I received a letter from my local hospital informing me that a bed was booked for me to have an operation on my right hand to repair the trigger finger. I had been having injections into my hand to no avail and was on the waiting list. I did not want to miss the opportunity of starting the course, yet on the other hand, the pain in my hand when writing or carrying out simple tasks was becoming unbearable. I put the situation to my line manager who suggested that I should have the operation.

Four days after the operation in the middle of the night when I was home alone, I suddenly woke up as if in a panic. I had only been asleep for one and a half hours. My heart was pounding and although there was no reason for me to feel afraid, I had a sense of fear overcoming me. I sat upright and checked my pulse under the bandage of my right hand. The rate was rapid and I noted that the rhythm was irregular. I felt that something was not quite right and found myself saying the strangest prayer. I said, "Heavenly Father, I am not afraid of dying but if You are going to take me to be with You tonight, please allow me to empty my bladder so that I would not be found lying in a pool of urine and also to unlock the front door so that the children would not have the expense of repairing it if it had to be broken into in order to get to me."

Clad in nightdress and dressing gown, I went to the bathroom then proceeded to go downstairs and unlock the front door leaving it on the latch. I prayed silently all the while thanking God for each minute I was still alive. I felt that the priority was to ring for an ambulance before trying to get hold of Josh and Vikki, something that could be done later. It was about one fifteen a.m. when I rang for the ambulance. The person on the other end of the telephone kept me in conversation with her until the paramedics arrived fifteen minutes later at about one thirty. I was taken to the ambulance where an electrocardiogram was performed and the results indicated that my heart, beating at the rate of one hundred and fifty four beats a minute was in severe atrial fibrillation which is an irregular, rapid heartbeat. The normal average heart rate is sixty-eight beats a minute. I was told that I had to be taken to hospital immediately.

On arrival at the hospital, I was taken to the casualty department where heart monitor leads were placed on my chest, arms and ankles; blood was taken for investigations and an intravenous infusion in my arm was commenced. This infusion contained a drug to assist the heart in returning to its normal rate and rhythm. There was a lot going on around me but I asked no questions until I was quickly taken on the trolley, moved to another area and noted that above the door, which we went through, was written 'Resuscitation Bay'. I looked up at the doctor and timidly asked, "Are you taking me to the resuscitation bay because I am going to die?" With a reassuring smile he said, "No, you are not going to die. The casualty department was a bit crowded and we have to remove the infusion from your arm and re-site it in your groin, otherwise you could lose your arm." Although I felt at peace, I was concerned that the children, up to this time had no idea what was happening to me.

Once the infusion was re-sited, I was moved to the rapid assessment unit where I spent approximately fours hours until six o'clock when a bed was available for me on the coronary care unit. Just before I was transferred to the coronary care unit, I asked the nurse to get in touch with Josh, Vikki and Karl. Unfortunately, she was unable to speak to them and left a message on each voicemail. Karl was the first to pick up his message and arrived at the hospital that morning at ten o'clock. The children eventually rang the hospital and were informed of my condition.

I spent the following three days 'attached' to the cardiac monitor so that my heart rate could be easily monitored. I commenced anti-coagulant therapy to keep me from developing blood clots and as a result had to have my blood taken daily for checking the clotting levels. My arms were covered in bruises over the sites that were used for taking my blood. Despite treatment, my heart rate remained in atrial fibrillation and on the morning of the third day when the doctors assessed my condition on the ward round, it was suggested that if my heart remained in atrial fibrillation, I would have to have my heart defibrillated by electric shock. On the morning of the fourth day, in answer to prayer, my heart righted itself and later that day I was discharged on medication which included injections to self-administer into my abdomen.

Having been discharged on Thursday, I was able to attend my lectures on Friday but was unable to work on the wards because my right hand remained bandaged. On the following Monday when I went to my GP for a repeat prescription of the tablets for my heart condition, it was noted that my heart rate was very low and I was told that I should be seen in the casualty department of the hospital immediately. I was again admitted to the coronary care unit for further investigations and discharged the following day. Two weeks later I was re-admitted for a further four days for the same condition.

However, I was determined to attend University and as a result did not miss any lectures. At the end of the six-month period, I was successful in completing the course and following an interview, was accepted for the post of midwife; a post which brought with it many challenges but was indeed, a fulfilling and eye-opening experience. Among the many members of staff with whom I worked, I had the privilege of meeting Denise, Gifty Gift and Savi who have now been added to my list of valued friends. My aim was to continue employment until the age of sixty-five but owing to ill health, I was forced to take early retirement just two weeks before my sixtieth birthday.

CONCLUSION

During his visit to the United Kingdom in 2005, my father and I had the opportunity to discuss the effects the trauma of my upbringing had on me. He was oblivious to how I had been affected but remorseful. It was a time of forgiving and putting the past behind us. Also, since my divorce from Karl, he and I have developed a unique friendship which has blossomed.

My life experiences related in this book are not exceptional; in fact, they represent some of the weaknesses of ordinary, normal people in everyday circumstances. However, what I have discovered is that God who created the heavens and the earth, who is God of all gods, Lord of all lords, King of all kings and who is sovereign Lord over my life, has sustained me through the trials written in this book and even much, much more. Through these experiences my faith and trust in God are being strengthened and I am learning to trust Him even when circumstances in life appear senseless, unjust and painful knowing that whatever happens His grace will always abound.

7

Lightning Source UK Ltd.
Milton Keynes UK
UKOW02f1224121115

262526UK00002B/9/P